FORGIVENESS IS FREEDOM

How I overcame life challenges to thrive and succeed, and YOU can too!

STEVEN BARENDREGT

Copyright © 2022 Steve Barendregt

All rights reserved. No part of this publication may be reproduced, distributed, or transmitted in any form or by any means, including photocopying, recording, or other electronic, or mechanical methods, without the prior written permission of the author or publisher, except in the case of brief quotations embodied in reviews and certain other non-commercial uses permitted by copyright law.

This publication is designed to provide accurate and authoritative information regarding the subject matter covered. It is sold with the understanding that the author or publisher is not engaged in rendering legal, accounting, or other professional services. If legal advice or other expert assistance is required, the services of a competent professional person should be sought.

Print ISBN: 978-1-7387791-0-9
Ebook ISBN: 978-1-7387791-3-0

Cover Image: @jodiarmitphotography | Jodi Armit

Printed in Canada

I dedicate this book to my siblings: Gord Pierson, Bill Pierson, Sandi (Sue) Cadeau, Dan Pierson and Larry Barendregt. We've all been through this journey in one way or another; each of us having our own stories. But a common bond has been our love for our mother Joyce (Hoskin) Pierson. Let her memory hold us together which was always her lasting wish.

YOUR FREE GIFT!

As a thank you for reading my book, I'd love to invite you to download the accompanying Affirmations Journal. This journal has affirmations, journal prompts and quotes pulled from the book that are designed to help you reflect on your own journey.

You can claim your complimentary copy here
www.bookstomotivate.com/journal

TRIGGER WARNING

This book contains swear words, words and accounts of domestic violence, suicide, and death of a parent.

Please engage in self-care as you read this book.

TABLE OF CONTENTS

Foreword xi
Chapter 1: From Rubber Boots To Boardroom 1
Chapter 2: I Never Really Knew My Father 9
Chapter 3: An Orphanage Is Not A Home 17
Chapter 4: The Moment and The Egg 25
Chapter 5: Outside the Door Looking In 29
Chapter 6: Adopted Again? 37
Chapter 7: In Chaos, I Find My Centre 43
Chapter 8: The Universe Found Me in The Rye Field 67
Chapter 9: Go Forward, Even If You Don't Know Why 71
Chapter 10: A Product Of Our Environment? 79
Chapter 11: Tobacco: I Ain't A Quitter 85
Chapter 12: A Little Help From My Friends 91
Chapter 13: From Eggshells to Ice Cream 113
Chapter 14: I'm High on Life, Not Drugs 119
Chapter 15: Nurturing a Seedling Teaches You About Life 133
Chapter 16: Farming Hope and Dreams 139
Chapter 17: Starting Over Can Be Powerful 149
Chapter 18: Creating Possibilities 159
Chapter 19: Shedding The Past 167
Chapter 20: I Really Don't Have a Need For Anyone Else 171
Chapter 21: Be Brave and Create 187
Chapter 22: Forgiveness Is Freedom 195
Epilogue 199
Acknowledgements 203
About The Author 205

FOREWORD

He grabbed my head, told me to close my mouth. Pressing my lips together, he proceeded to use the black eyeliner and wrote across my entire mouth the word, "FILTH."

"If you wash this off at any time during school, I will kill you."

Steve Barendregt is one of nearly eight billion people on the planet. His story is about as unique as any I've ever read. It's resplendent in its unapologetically raw innocent account of an upbringing not many of us could fathom. Yet it remains relatable. No parent of mine ever expressed their anger by writing on my face; but still, I can feel the humiliation and the suffering.

By the age of seven, Steve had lost both of his parents; his mom to cancer and his dad to alcohol and correctional services.

Did he ever have a chance? And if so, how?

Before she died, Steve's mom wrote her six children a note that he would read for the rest of his life. Closing his eyes and inhaling the letter, all he could hope for was a fragrance that would remind him of a love that never left him. Studying the handwriting, he tried desperately to recapture her personality, even if only for a moment.

We should all stop saying how amazing it is that mothers know their children. Of course they do. Even if Steve was only seven when his mom wrote that note, she captured his essence in a few short sentences. But she wasn't the only one that knew the real Steve; there was one other person.

It's fitting that the backdrop of Steve's story occurs in the farming belt of rural Ontario; a land that's both fertile and unforgiving. When you're a farmer, you get to know life and death pretty well. You realize darn quickly that growth depends on nurturing. Without it, there are only weeds and dead crops. The seasons reflect an unrelenting cycle that brings hope and harvest for part of the year, while the remaining months are desolate and show no signs of mercy. It takes fortitude and belief to make something grow - especially self-worth.

Who could have known Steve as well as his mom? It wouldn't be the man that hurled a beer stein at his face, cutting Steve's chin wide open on the night of his speaking contest. And it wouldn't be the woman who made him sleep in a bathtub for a week. Nor would it be his siblings who were enduring their own hardships in their new home. That would leave only one person.

To know oneself is surprisingly uncommon. Most people define themselves by their careers, how many kids they have, their marital status, or where they live. They give little thought to what lies beneath the veneer. Today, between the barrage of social media content and our busy lives, there's little time for self-discovery. But in-between the grueling work on the farm and the instinct to avoid eye contact with his adopted parents, Steve was aware of a substratum; a layer beneath the veneer in which his true essence resided. It had always existed, from the moment he raised enough money to buy his dying mom a gift for Easter, and especially when he spoke with God in a rye field and discovered something profound; something altogether inspiring.

Steve was the one person who knew Steve.

As a ward of the Province, young Steve always saw himself on the outside, looking in. Perhaps that vantage point was a blessing rather than a curse since it instilled in him a desire to *want* to look inside. It would seem that whenever Steve trusted his instincts; whenever he ventured inside his own heart, the truth would reveal itself.

Steve's memoir is indeed a revealing journey. It's told in the first person, at times from the eyes of an innocent child, wanting nothing more than to be loved. Yet it often reads like a swashbuckling epic, moving from one incredible adventure to the next. It might also be described as a Dickensian tale, complete with malevolent characters acting as foils to the protagonist's growing feeling that he deserved more. At other times, the voice changes to a more experienced narrator, evaluating the heartache and objectively noting the lessons learned and the motivations behind Steve the child's actions.

I'm in a unique position, having mentored Steve on the writing of his memoir. My partner, Marcy Barbaro and I, spent countless evenings evaluating Steve's work, challenging him, teaching him the mechanics and the mindset of great book writing. Yet we both concur that as much as we taught, we were gifted the precious lessons inherent in Steve's experience. Humbly, we'd both say that we received far more than we could ever have given. And to boot, Steve transformed himself into a true author; not surprisingly, from which the etymology tells us is the word, *auctor*, which translates from Latin, *"father, creator, one who brings about, one who makes or creates."*

Upon reading Steve's story, the creator designation will become obvious; he's the creator of all that he's accomplished. He was the one person who had the intuition to look inside and know that he had, he'd always had, the power to create his future.

Steve's book is more than a fascinating story. It's the vulnerable sharing of the traumas that bind us as humans. Who hasn't experienced abuse, either first-hand or through someone close to us? Who hasn't lost something or someone so close to our hearts? To live is to experience; to experience is to live. It is a gift that we should all be so fortunate to share; the livingness that is our story. When we share, when we open our hearts; we grow together.

As you contemplate the life of Steve Barendregt in this incredible story of resilience and determination, you're bound to understand something that will defy your common sense: You'll observe and become part of a perspective that, right until the end, is forgiving. Though you'll feel the pain of verbal and physical abuse, the guilt and shame associated with the tribulations of a fellow human being, and the suffering Steve endured; you'll also feel the love. And when love is present, it always reverberates.

Love features prominently in this work, harmonizing with neglect and vengeful behaviour. It's the coat hanger on which every costume hangs; it's the humanity on which Steve's actions are pinned. Steve's love, a love that's sometimes apparent and other times buried like the farmlands in the winter, only to be uncovered in the spring, is a constant. Its bright light (and sometimes faint flame) attract a cast of characters that serve as counterpoints to the negative energy that swirls in and out of Steve's life. There is hope and light at the same time as there is the darkness of oppression.

And what you'll further discover, I won't divulge; because that's the treasure that awaits you in a story that's riveting, thought-provoking, and a testament to belief.

I'm privileged to have been a part of Steve's recollection of his childhood and the honest account of his journey. I'll be forever grateful to have gleaned the wisdom inherent in the lessons that appear in the latter part of Steve's book. But without the backstory - the context - the lessons would never have resonated to the extent that they do today. I wouldn't have been as profoundly touched as I've been without knowing what young Steve endured and how he held-on to something intangible, yet as real as the words you're reading right now. What he held onto for so long was a gift from the heart, which is precisely that which is this book: a gift from the heart.

You may be on the outside right now, but you're about to be let in.

~ Alex Morin, July 2022
alex@workingwriters.co

Chapter 1

FROM RUBBER BOOTS TO BOARDROOM

I can still see my mother standing on the porch with such a big smile and yelling laughingly, "Stevie, you're going to be sore walking like that."

I didn't care.

It was my first day of school in 1968. It was raining, but that didn't matter because I was wearing my new rubber boots. The boots with the yellow felt lining and army green rubber exterior.

They were brand new, and not a hand-me-down from my older brothers; which was normally the case in our family. My new boots were going to stay new…..forever! I walked the several blocks to school on my heels in an attempt to keep them clean.

My mother was tall and slender. Having been sick for so many years, it would have been impossible for her to be anything but. Though I was always afraid I wouldn't be able to remember her face after she was gone, I can still see her naturally reddish auburn hair.

That was the colour she wore when she died. I remember that because it's etched into my mind, after peering into her coffin so many years ago.

Her hair was never long, but she had curls. Her skin was porcelain soft. I still long to feel her soft hands on my face. I don't remember the colour of her eyes. The only pictures I have of her today are black and whites so I'll never see them again. My sister, thankfully, reminds me that they were hazel and so I'm grateful for that. Her smile was big and beautiful. I miss that.

Back in those days, kindergarten class was only half a day. I used to walk home for lunch and Mom would be waiting for me. One of my fondest memories was watching *The Edge of Night* (a soap opera) on the black & white TV set. The best part for me was curling up to her while watching it. I don't remember the program, but I was so happy and warm being with her by myself. Life was good. I felt safe. At five years old, isn't that the way we should all feel?

Mom was gone from my life by the time I was seven. Even in that short time, I never doubted her love. She set the tone for what would benchmark all future role models in my life.

I was the fifth of six children; five boys and one sister. My earliest recollection of childhood was a mix of emotions; many of which I recall being happy, as long as Mom was nearby.

But that wasn't always the case. I was born Stephen John Henry Pierson on June 23, 1963. Mom died on May 14, 1971. When Mom died, she was thirty-one years of age with six children, ages five to twelve. I really didn't have a lot of time for bonding; much less understanding what the hell was happening to my life after she died. How does a seven year old even start to put thoughts together to make any sense of the death of his mother?

I looked to my five siblings for safety, for comfort; God, for ANYTHING that would make the pain go away.

I wanted to make my brothers and sister laugh again too. I reverted to being as funny as possible. It seemed to work. I used humour to drown out the pain for myself and my siblings too. Because I seemed to develop a penchant for talking, the humour came easily. I learned to read at a young age. By age five, I would read everything in sight. I created funny anecdotes in my head from the words I read on street signs, park signs, buses; and just about everywhere. I used those words to make my siblings laugh.

Having a way with words at such a young age was a good thing. Not being able to understand the words I read and the sentences I'd create got me into trouble..

One day my brother was truly bugging me. He was relentless, and I became furious with him.

So, I blurted out "Billy, you're just a bugger."

This was within earshot of my mother and she ran into the room and scolded me for using foul language. I pleaded not to be sent to my room. I tried explaining to her that Billy was bugging me a lot and so he was a *bugger*; not understanding this was deemed a swear word. Perhaps it was lower on the scale of profanities but still a profanity, nonetheless, for a five year-old.

Years later, when I think about this story and maintain that the crime didn't fit the punishment, I realize how my mother must have seen it then. There must have been so many life lessons to teach all six of us kids, knowing she was dying of cancer. So little time. In retrospect, I praise her for taking exception to her five year-old boy using such language.

We were a welfare family. Mom didn't work. How could she when she was regularly undergoing treatment for cancer? And when she wasn't getting treatment, she was recovering, and certainly not well enough to work.

Cancer had plagued my maternal family for seven or eight decades. It was and is *Familial Adenomatous Polyposis (FAP)*. It's a condition that triggers the growth of cancerous polyps inside the bowel. It's an inherited gene fault or mutation that increases the risk of bowel cancer.

Mom's entire family on her mother's side also died from this disease. Her brother and sister had both succumbed to it at an early age too. My maternal grandmother had died when my mom was only five years old. Fortunately, she still had a caring father in her life at that time. Medical advances have slightly improved our family prospects of not dying so early from this disease. Regrettably, it hasn't been eliminated. Of the six siblings, the two oldest boys inherited the mutated gene and have had multiple surgeries to remove the cancerous polyps. I'm grateful they're still here.

Naturally, growing up, I worried about whether or not I had the same gene. Would I too die young from the same affliction? Death became a preoccupation for me from an early age. In a strange way, it was comforting because I felt closer to Mom when I was thinking about death. I recall praying to her often, and she heard me, hoping somehow, she would appear to me. A seven year-old just trying to put it all together; the shattered pieces of my young life.

Because of the genetic risk of this cancer, from the age of thirteen, I would go to the hospital annually for a bowel scope. I'll never forget the first time I had this procedure. Back then, they never used a mild sedative to help with the process. Today, they usually do. Aside from the obvious, I was terrified. I remember the surgery nurse trying to calm me down. The doctor who performed these scopes was the same doctor who treated my mother. I felt safer with him because I knew he treated Mom.

Regardless, my first time through the ordeal was terrifying. I was sweating profusely, not knowing what was going to happen. The nurse was so understanding and did everything to calm me down as she could see that I was terrified. She was so empathetic; I wondered if she had known my mom.

When I was sixteen or seventeen, I was going in for my annual check up and scope. By now, I was used to the routine. Assume the same position; knees up and butt out. The doctor began with the scope and as unpleasant as it was, I knew it'd be over soon. I assumed, just like always, it was the doctor, a nurse and myself in the room.

Just then I heard the doctor say, "Ok class, come forward here and have a look."

My face went flush as I turned around to see four young students moving in for a look at ME! Three of the students were female and one in particular quite attractive, I recall.

"OH MY GOD!!" That was all I could say under my breath as I curled into a ball and hid my face from further embarrassment. I fully support coaching and learning, but perhaps not at the expense of my vulnerable sixteen year-old self. Perhaps this was my first lesson in humility.

By the time I reached my early thirties and had children of my own, I decided to take a genetic test at Mount Sinai hospital. This was to confirm whether or not I had the same gene that had cursed my family for so long. I also didn't want my own children to go through all that I had to if it could be avoided.

Again, I found myself in that familiar space of death. I began formulating a plan. What would I do if I had the gene? Had I put things in place to take care of my family? My kids were still young. I hadn't even had enough time with them. *This can't happen!* So many thoughts were going through my mind.

This genetic test was complex and took a very long time to complete. They had my brother Gord's genetic information to work from, and I'm told without that information, it could have taken even longer. I was surprised when the research doctor who worked on my case advised me that my genetic chain was very long. When I asked how long, she explained it was the length of two football fields. That was difficult for me to imagine.

Finally, two years later, I received a call from the hospital to come-in for the results. I was anxious because on the phone they asked me a question:

"If you have the gene, how would that make you feel?"

Selfishly, I thought, *What kind of question is that? Why are you asking me THAT question? Do you already know I have this gene and you're setting me up?*

In hindsight, it was a good question. I just didn't know it at the time.

After nearly eight hundred days, I received the results.

"You don't have the gene, Steven. How do you feel?"

After agreeing to having the test, that one question played in my mind for months. I played it over and over: If I had the gene, how would I tell my young family? I didn't want to die. I didn't want to leave my wife or my children; Lindsay and Matthew. How would I provide for them emotionally, financially?

It never occured to me that a negative test result would make me happy. That's how I viewed things in my life; it was always about everyone else. I think being exposed to so much sickness and death early in life, I just focused on taking care of those around me more than myself. That characteristic, albeit noble, would cause difficulties for me in the years ahead. At that moment, however, none of what I had contemplated was registering. My thoughts were all jumbled up.

"Steven, did you hear what I said?"

I was stunned.

"STEVEN, YOU DON'T HAVE THE GENE, THIS WILL NOT BE THE WAY YOU WILL DIE."

That's what I heard after I cleared my head. I was waiting to hear the opposite. I had all sorts of feelings going on in my heart and in my head.

I was happy. I was sad. I felt guilty.

I was angry. "WHAT DO YOU MEAN I DON'T HAVE WHAT MY MOM HAD?"

I finally came to understand the message, but I just wanted to get out of there. I needed to be alone.

How was I ever going to be able to tell my older brothers Gord and Bill? Both Bill and Gord had the gene. Both had endured a number of surgeries already. In fact, I was taken back to the day when brother Bill was only thirteen years old. He came home from his first surgery with a hole in his gut. That sight alone impacted me. It was scary, gross and confusing all mixed together for me. How did that make brother Bill feel? Imagine; a thirteen year old being told he has cancerous polyps that need to be removed. God! It makes me shudder even now.

I grabbed the report and darted out of there as fast as I could. I got outside and took a deep breath. Standing in the parking lot at the hospital, I started bawling.

I felt somehow that I'd betrayed my brothers. I wanted this fucking gene because in some way I thought I would be closer to Mom; have a part of her inside of me, no matter how bad it was. What the fuck was I thinking? That's when my anger showed up. After all these years, the emotions poured out of me. I was dizzy with emotion.

Suddenly, I heard a voice from the distance, then louder:

"Are you ok, Sir?"

Thankfully, that person's voice brought me back from what I'm sure would have been a complete breakdown.

I composed myself. I got in my car and just sat there collecting my thoughts. At the time, I had a mobile car phone supplied to me by my employer.

I dialed Gord. He picked-up and I started crying. I felt so guilty telling him that I didn't have the gene. I told him how I wanted to have it to be closer to Mom.

Gord stopped me from ranting with a simple, "I love you, Bro."

It was EVERYTHING at that moment. It was reassuring. In a simple phrase, he erased my guilt, my anger, my confusion.

Days later I read the actual report which I still have in my personal files.

DIAGNOSIS: "Steven Barendregt (#959) has not inherited the same truncating germline mutation that was identified in his brother (Gord) and therefore, is not at risk for FAP."

I learned to accept my fate in the years that followed, which would set me on a new path. I would eventually resolve to live my own life and not someone else's. Up until this point, I'd compartmentalized life as *"before Mom died," "at the orphanage"* or *"with the Barendregts."*

This would eventually all fade into the background to make room for me to live my own life.

CHAPTER 2

I NEVER REALLY KNEW MY FATHER

"I cannot think of any need in childhood as strong as the need for a father's protection" - Sigmund Freud

Mom rented our home at 927 Dufferin Ave., on the East side of London, Ontario. I've never forgotten that address. Years later, my brother Gord reminded me that Mom actually had a *"rent-to-own"* structure for many years. The cost of the house was $13,000 and she had been paying it off over the years. Unfortunately, when she died, all that she had paid was lost. What little she had left to finally pay it off did not get resolved, and no one else; including our old man, would ever have that kind of money. How truly regrettable, as I know it would have been a significant achievement for her to have been able to have that home to leave us kids.

As an adult, I found myself periodically driving by the house just to catch a feeling of how it used to be when Mom was alive. I don't think I ever felt Mom's presence, but I always came away with a sense of pride, knowing that I had built a life from the beginning of such simple means.

Measuring myself from where I came from drove me forward many times throughout my adult years. These days, I don't think of life in terms of better or worse. Life just is, was, and will be. I've come to realize that I've been growing, expanding and learning all these years. For no better or worse, I simply chose a path. I realized that was where the magic came from: deliberately choosing a path. That house is where *I* came from, and it's brought me to this very day. It's been a steady, progressive realization of my true self, ever since. I still cherish the memory of that house.

In 1987, I was a young new commercial banker when I purchased my very first home in London, Ontario. I had a great job, was newly married, and had a baby on the way. I mean, look at me. This kid from the orphanage, of meager beginnings. And look what I'd accomplished. Nevertheless, I quietly celebrated that moment and remembered saying a prayer of thanks. I secretly hoped Mom would be looking down with the same sense of pride. Funny enough, a wonderful event happened after I bought that house. I went across the street to help an elderly couple who had been struggling with an extension ladder. We introduced ourselves. Our conversation eventually led to where the woman had worked before recently retiring. She said she'd worked at an orphanage for years.

I asked her which one, and her answer made me choke. It was the same orphanage that my siblings and I had lived in. When I told her I was Stephen Pierson, she became very emotional. Her eyes flooded over with tears.

She asked, "Are you one of Joyce Pierson's kids?"

She smiled the biggest smile when I confirmed that I was.

She said, "I'd always wondered what ever happened to you six kids."

We talked for hours that afternoon.

Imagine, my new neighbour being one of my caretakers at the orphanage! She told me she was the one who cuddled me the day we were told of Mom's passing. In some small way I felt validated that day.

I was proud of where I was in life at that moment; literally and figuratively. I was living a life that little Stephen Pierson, from the orphanage, had never thought possible: a life I knew even this woman before me would never have thought possible. She knew the circumstances of us Pierson kids years before. Her reaction said it all. How could any of us ever have stood a chance?

Following Mom's passing, and as early as I can remember, I was looking for signs in life that would direct me on my path. Signs from Mom in heaven. It made me feel closer to her. I was using these signs to survive in some way. Meeting that woman must have been one of those signs. That day was a gift.

My earliest memories begin at the age of four or five. I haven't spoken of our father yet because he wasn't in our lives very much; only in and out, at times.

My dad wasn't a big man. In fact, I dare say he wasn't more than five feet, eight inches tall. He had a dashing smile. I had heard stories over the years of how all the ladies were enchanted by him. He had thick dark hair that was slicked back. Even when he died his hair was still thick and slicked back, but gray. His voice was distinguishably raspy, which no doubt came from the years of boozing and heavy smoking. He always had a cigarette in his hand and just as frequently, a bottle of beer.

During this time of my life, I really only have two memories of Dad, whose name was Larry.

One afternoon walking home from school, a big rig truck came roaring up the street and stopped at the curb. The gigantic door swung open and there he was with a big smile and, like always, his cigarette pressed between his lips.

He said, "Stevie, you wanna ride?"

That was way too cool for me. I was never as proud of my dad as that day, I think. He was almost hero-like to me in that big truck.

I think he knew it as well and took every advantage to act the part for me. He hoisted me by the arm all the way up to the cab and the big rig seat. It was only a few more blocks home, but that ride was so much fun for me. I still remember the air brakes making that *hissing* sound. To this day, I still love it when I hear air brakes applied on the trucks. It reminds me of Dad. I also liked the big steering wheel. I recall sitting on his lap. The steering wheel was soft and smooth.

I still like big rig steering wheels to this day too. The wafting of his cigarette in the cab, the roar of the engine, and the country music blaring in the speakers all made for a very memorable ride. Despite all the issues I may have had with my dad for not being a part of my life, I wish he was here today so I could describe how that made me feel and to thank him. He may have known how happy I was because my smile was as big as my belly. I hope he noticed that.

The other memory was when Larry came home drunk. As best as I can remember, he was always drinking; always had a beer in his hand. He would drink day and night and start all over again the next day.

With his drunkenness, an argument ensued between him and my mother. At the time, I didn't know what caused the argument. Later in life, I learned it was because he had drunk away Mom's "baby bonus" cheque. We had little money as it was, and now Mom had no grocery money for the six of us kids. She was crying profusely.

Well, the argument was taken outside on the front lawn. It wasn't long before the whole street of neighbours were lined up watching what was going on. Oddly enough, all of us kids were there too with Mom. I can still hear the beer bottle "crack" when it hit the old man's hand after my Mom flung it at him. I remember wondering why so many people were standing around instead of helping poor Mom.

I remember feeling really embarrassed for all of us.

Even at that young age, I had a sense of deserving a better life.

Why did we have to live like this?

I Never Really Knew My Father

How does a five year-old even know how to think like that? I did. I knew I didn't like how I felt when all the chaos and crying was happening. I believe, to this day, I was driven by a desire to want more. I knew I deserved it.

I know keeping six kids fed must have been a worry for our mother, but she was resourceful. I never recall feeling hungrier than happy when she was alive.

Back then, bread was cheap and filling. Our breakfast cereal was broken bread pieces with milk and lots of sugar added to it. I never liked it much, but the sugar helped it go down, and I didn't want Mom to feel bad about it. To this day for me, any resemblance of soggy bread turns my stomach! It's precisely these experiences that taught me to be empathetic to others who are less fortunate. As such, I give to charities that help those in need and to single mothers and children in particular. Family sit-down meals are important to me, and I'm especially proud of the large harvest table that we have in our cottage. It was intentionally meant to accommodate many to join together, to eat and be happy.

I learned later in life that my father was a habitual drunk. Part of his life involved petty crimes; crimes that were bad enough to land him in the local jail; and later, Kingston Penitentiary. I think he stole things and was known to "kite" cheques. Kiting is a form of fraud. But in any event, my recollection of Dad was of him being in jail more often than being with us.

I can't say I ever really knew my father. I don't think I saw him after Mom died until I was well into my adulthood. I find it amazing how blood is thicker than water though. Regardless of how little I knew him, when I was old enough to make my own decisions, I wanted to meet him again. At least as an adult, I could decide for myself what kind a man he was.

As it turns out, he was still an alcoholic in my adult years. I know that old habits are pretty hard to break. And he never stopped smoking either.

One year, he went to the hospital to get help with his drinking so I guess there was a time he thought about getting better.

While I visited him in the hospital, I asked his doctor, "What kind of a person is my dad?"

He told me he was brilliant. I thought he was joking. The doctor went on to say that out of one hundred people in a room, his God-gifted mentality would be in the top four. He explained to me that as a result of his drinking, as well as him being in the prison system for so many years, he was socially inept. I had heard rumours from my older brothers, who knew him better than I ever did, that he was very smart and could build or do anything with his hands. What a shame, I thought. All that talent wasted for so many years. What could he have done if he had found another path? Great things, I'll bet.

We never did attempt to develop a father-son bond in those later years, but I think that was best and likely easier for both of us. I did, however, learn to give him the respect I would give any other elder, and I afforded him more leniency than I would anyone else who wasn't my biological father.

In spite of all the hurt, I introduced him to my daughter Lindsay when she was around three to four years of age. From that visit, I gave him a picture of him holding his granddaughter. It must have meant a lot to him, because I was pleasantly surprised when he kept that picture with him. I knew that he cared enough by that simple act. I received it back after he died.

I spent one evening with him while we both visited my brother Larry. In fact, I "bunked" with him in a tent in Larry's backyard that night. I tried to ask him questions about memories of Mom, but I knew he didn't want to talk much about it. I have no doubt he loved her. I have no doubt he loved all of us, but he wasn't capable of loving the way I had expected it to be between us.

I Never Really Knew My Father

I received a call from my brother in 1999: "Dad's not well and he probably won't make it."

Despite not really having any sort of relationship with the man, nothing would keep me away from being with him at that time. I stayed with him those last few days in the hospital. My siblings and I comforted him and watched over him. I know it felt good, for him and for us, to have all of his children at his bedside, until his end. Even Mom didn't have that fortune. I was doing it partially for him, but mostly for the memory of our mother. I buried his ashes with his mother and father at the foot of their tombstone. He was sixty. I wish I had taken more time to ask him questions. There was so much I wanted to know and so much that remains a mystery to me, to this day.

Chapter 3

AN ORPHANAGE IS NOT A HOME

"Where can we hide in fair weather, we orphans of the storm?"- Evelyn Waugh

When Mom was feeling better and not undergoing cancer treatment, she would be home with us. When Mom invariably took ill again, she went back to the hospital and we were sent back to the orphanage. I didn't know it then, but we were officially Wards of the Province. A ward is a child who's placed under the protection of a legal guardian and is the legal responsibility of the government. I remember we had a case worker from the Children's Aid Society (CAS). They would come to see us periodically; and when mom was healthy enough to be home, they would come talk with her at the house.

Despite being a crown ward, when my dad was out of jail, he had custody of us. That meant, where he lived, we went with him. To be fair to him, I never really felt afraid or threatened by being with him. With his drinking buddies and the way he was, it was a care-free party-like environment.

Thinking of this in my adult years, giving him custody of us made no sense at all. Why would the CAS put us in his "care," knowing his troubles and how he lived? I know it must have been a challenge with all six of us kids at the orphanage, but I would expect more from the CAS.

There was a time in my adult years when I was angry at the CAS for not paying more attention to us. Though I had become quite familiar with anger in my older years, I eventually let that feeling go. I could have been mad at the whole world, but in fairness, I really didn't know any better. I just knew I wanted a better life; even then.

Looking back, I find it rather amazing that, at such a young age, I was developing fundamental leadership skills. These skills would benefit me greatly in the years ahead. It was my way to survive in an environment that would have extinguished me if I hadn't wanted more for myself. These skills would help me to find my way out of a toxic environment that I wasn't even aware of at this point; but one that would present itself to me in the future.

Because we moved around between the orphanage, home, or wherever Larry housed us, I had to attend several different schools in grades one and two. That was a challenge. I missed a lot of the fundamental teachings in those two grades, which hindered me in later years. My mathematics skills suffered the most and spoiler alert: I became a banker!

Moving around so much taught me how to adapt quickly, fit in quietly, and read people well. I labelled myself, even at a young age, as being "street-smart." I've often said that despite so many challenges in my early years, they were often lessons that helped me in my later years. They helped me meet people, build trust with people, relate to others and more.

There were two different orphanages in London, Ontario that we went to. Heck knows why we went to one over the other. But it likely had to do with fitting six kids in one home together, I'd have to think.

The first orphanage we went to I will refer to as "The Rough House." In my view, this home most closely represented how dysfunctional our lives were. It was consistent with the way we lived.

The "Rough House" was looser in terms of strict guidelines that you might expect for children as young as we were. I was about four and five years old at that time. Sexual intercourse amongst the teens was a regular sighting, and profanities were a normal part of our vocabulary. It was a sort of free-for-all in every respect, and I'm certain had I been one of the many teens in there at that time I would have impregnated a girl, been in jail, or both.

The first day we arrived at "the Rough House," was a day my oldest brother Gord will never forget, I'm sure. Moving from one place to another and learning to fit-in was becoming the norm; but wow, this would be a test.

Gord had to stand up to represent the "Pierson Clan" by running through a line up of kids, getting banged and bumped all the way through, kind of like a pinball game. The good news is that only Gord was put through the test. Because of Gord, the rest of us Pierson kids were accepted on our new turf. I've never asked him his thoughts on that experience, but I know he would have protected us in any way he could. We younger kids counted on that.

Though my brother Dan will remember this story better than I do, it'll provide a sense of how uncontrolled and dysfunctional this orphanage often was. One day, we piled into a station wagon with one of the counselors driving us to some outing. When it was time to head home, my brother and I were already in the car waiting. One of the older kids from the orphanage clocked the counsellor, stole the car keys, and drove off.

Don't forget: my brother and I were in that car when this happened. I remember how exciting it was as police cars with flashing lights chased us like we were in an action movie! I learned, years later, that the young man driving the car was trying to get back to his home on the native reserve. Once he hit that line, they would have been out of police jurisdiction and the chase would have come to a stop. Tragic, isn't it? In the end, we were returned safely and I'm sure the young man was in a heap of trouble.

On another outing, we visited the Detroit Zoo. We all piled in a bus, and away we went. I really enjoyed the zoo; so much so that I can still remember everyone hanging around the orangutan cages watching them play and be silly. I was so captivated, watching.

The next thing I remember was looking around and noticing that my group had disappeared. It wasn't long until I was crying, and someone came to my aid. I ended-up at the police station, so afraid and sick to my stomach from fear, that I even turned down offers of candy, pop, and potato chips. It turns out that the person responsible for the head count double-counted my brother who looked a lot like me. Days later, when all was back to normal, I sure wished I had taken all that candy they'd offered me then.

The last orphanage we went to was different. I'll refer to it as "The Safe House." It was orderly and had a set of strict rules. I preferred the order that came with this orphanage. I remember feeling safer, happier, and more secure there. Without realizing it then, I chose that structure for how I would build my own life, in later days. Order makes me comfortable; I dislike being out of control. I suppose it's a form of self-protection. Turns out, it worked for me and it kept me on the right path, for the most part.

The Safe House always felt safer in a variety of ways. The staff wore something similar to nurses uniforms, and they had a lot of rules. These rules were nothing out of the ordinary for children under twelve, which all of us Pierson kids were at that time. After dinner, each night, we'd have a bath, in which they'd wash our hair with vinegar. I thought it was weird. I learned that it was to improve scalp health and likely stave off lice. Right after the bath we went to bed.

The Safe House was located near the hospital where Mom stayed. I still remember the squeak of the nurses' running shoes on the polished floor as they patrolled the halls while we were meant to be sleeping in our beds. The rooms were almost institutional or hospital-like. I had my own closet, night stand, and my own bed which was much different than sharing a room, or a bed with my brothers. Nevertheless, I longed to be home with my brothers and sister and especially to be with Mom.

As an adult, building my life, I used to drive by the orphanage frequently. It provided me an opportunity to reflect; to remind me where I came from. When my children were older, I would drive them past The Safe House, where I once lived.

My bedroom window faced the road. I would say, "There's Daddy's old bedroom." I wanted my kids to know how well they had it in life and to recognize those who were less fortunate. As adults, my children give to charities whenever they can.

Indulge me here as I share a few more great memories with Mom and all of my siblings together. In the upbringing I had, you either had to laugh or to cry in order to cope. Call it the grace of God, my natural disposition, or dumb luck, but I learned to laugh and make light of difficulties. And it has served me well.

At 927 Dufferin Avenue, we had one of the biggest backyards on the street. Many baseball games were played there. I learned to ride a bicycle against the curb. Gord and Bill had propped me up on a bike that was way too big for me and cheered when I finally got going on my own. We made our own fun and many days we had a lot of it. I'm sure it was during these times with my siblings that I developed a sense of humour. I don't have to tell you how much humour took the edge off and helped me cope with the things I didn't understand as a kid.

As you will learn later in this book, the tightness of my family, the fun we had, and good survival instincts, helped me grow my entrepreneurial spirit. That actually began when I was six years old. As you now know, we had little money. We had to learn to survive, often on our own, and to this day I cannot believe how I pulled this off.

Back in the 60's, kids played outside a lot more than they do now. We had a lot of freedom given our situation. It was nothing to walk the six or ten blocks from our home to downtown. That's where the infamous Western Fair was held every fall.

I loved the fair; especially the food and the candy. Of course, not having any money, I hungrily sought a way to get some (candy, that is). The local dry cleaner on Dundas Street was owned by a man who I recall had a thick accent of some sort. I think European or even Russian, because I can still hear the echo of his voice:

"You bring me coat hangers, I pay two pennies for each."

WOW, I thought. *"I'm in the money,"* because I knew we had some hangers at home and all I had to do was race home and get them.

I ran as fast as my little legs would carry me, charged through the front door, and went to every closet and grabbed them to take back. I didn't even know enough to straighten them up nicely to make them easier to carry. I had what I thought was a fortune, but was really a messy heap of wires. I think the shop owner was as surprised as I was at how fast I came back with those hangers.

He roared out a big guttural laugh and said," You make money fast little one," and he handed me two whole dimes.

Well, twenty cents back then was the start of my little empire.

I then told some of my neighbours about my new venture. You wouldn't believe it, but it wasn't long before the ladies, all of whom likely knew our "family situation," set out their hangers on their porches for me to come pick up. Each of them even neatly bundled them together with twist ties and elastics. I walked up and down both sides of the street with my wagon gathering them, and counted the money at every bundle I stacked. I can't remember how long this continued, but I do remember that year at the Western Fair I was a king! My brother Dan and I enjoyed burgers, fries, and even a milkshake.

Whether it was entrepreneurial instinct or just survival, it doesn't matter. It built confidence in thinking that, one day, I could take care of Mom. That was the end plan: Stevie the caretaker; a characteristic I learned as a result of Mom's constant poor health that stays with me to this day.

These lessons, and God only knows where they came from, formed a lasting spirit that helped me as I grew up. I often have friends say how bad it must have been. But I say that I learned how to survive. I learned how to be resourceful; to adapt quickly, read people well and, ultimately, develop a trustworthy personality and a reputation for being genuinely likeable. Without so many of these hardships, I would not be who I am today.

Chapter 4

THE MOMENT AND THE EGG

It was always exciting when we got to go see Mom at the hospital. While I didn't know it then, this would be the last hospital visit with her. It was around Easter-time, 1971. We all wanted to give Mom something special of course. I walked blocks to the local department store on Dundas Street; *Woolworth's*, I think, to see what we could find. A "luck-of-the-draw" activity we all learned was checking the phone booth change slot, just in-case there happened to be change there. On that particular day, I raced to get there first, and sure enough, a whole quarter! What luck, I thought. It allowed me to do something that has stuck with me to this day.

The store had one of those hollow chocolate Easter Eggs on the shelf. Do you remember the kind? It was the one that had the pink icing swirl on top and I figured it'd be the perfect gift for Mom. I don't remember the cost but that extra 25 cents from the phone booth went towards, what I thought, was the world's most amazing gift. If I recall correctly, the store keeper, upon hearing why I needed *that* particular egg, allowed me to short-pay the cost.

That particular visit with Mom was special because she seemed so happy. She even had enough strength to pull herself up with her overhead bar and sit up straight in her bed. All of us were eager to give our gifts to her. I could hardly wait because I was so sure THIS was the best one of all, even though I can't tell you what my siblings presented her with that day.

Easter, 1971 fell on April 11th. We likely would have visited Mom on the Saturday because "Grandma" would have had to attend church on the Sunday. I should mention here that "Grandma," in this case, was Pat. She married my Grandfather Charles "Ivan" Hoskin. She was my mom's step-mother, since I mentioned earlier that her mother had died when she was only five. For all my life she was "Grandma" and she deserves more than a minor mention in this book, if I'm being fair. Four weeks after having presented Mom with the greatest Easter gift of all (or so I thought), she died. That was on Friday May 14th, 1971.

Grandma came to visit us at The Safe House orphanage the following day; a Saturday. I remember being excited and asking her how Mommy was.

She said, "Well, that's what I was going to tell you about."

We all proceeded into a private office.

"Well kids, I'm so sorry but Mommy has died and gone to heaven."

I don't think I heard her right because the first person I looked at was my brother Dan who was closest to me in age. And when he started crying; so did I. I knew something was wrong but I was only seven and those words just weren't making any sense.

I remember we were asked to go outside in the playground to do whatever. That's when I climbed the big steel slide in the playground. I must have blacked out because I fell right off the top of the ladder onto the hard ground below. It knocked me unconscious and I only remember the odd feeling of not being able to get up. When I came around, I cried my eyes out for what seemed like forever.

I was told by Grandma that I was too young to go to the funeral. Years later, I regretted her decision, but perhaps it was right. I remember the funeral home visitation. I remember what Mom wore and how her hair looked. I remember the smell of the flowers. To this day, I detest the smell of mums because that smell brings me back to her funeral. I guess

Grandma was right in her decision not to allow me to attend the funeral. I had nightmares about my mom's casket for years.

In the days that followed I remember Grandma brought us a box of Mom's belongings that I guess she thought we might want to have.

I will never forget the pit in my stomach, the lump in my throat, and the deep anxiety when I looked in the box. I saw THAT Easter egg; the one I had given her. I was mortified.

Everything raced through my mind.

Why didn't she eat her egg? Didn't she really like it? Did she love me?

I was heartbroken. How could I ever be able to tell her I loved her again?

Everything welled-up inside and I wept. Looking back, I believe this was *the moment*. This would have been the pivotal moment in which I instantly inherited a fear of abandonment; a topic I'll elaborate upon later in this book.

In a solitary moment, a part of my innocence was erased. It was sobering. Life was NOT good anymore. I felt lost and afraid.

Why had this happened to us? Who was going to take care of us?

For me, "Stevie, the funny clown" learned the hard way that life wasn't always funny; a lesson I would hear in the days ahead, from the grave, through a letter Mom had written to us children prior to her death.

Following Mom's death, there must have been a need for the orphanage to find a more permanent situation for us Pierson kids. Our mother's wish was to keep us all together. As an adult I realized just how difficult that would have been; especially given that none of us were babies any longer. Most adoptive parents are searching for a newborn baby. As the second youngest in the family, I had a lot of foster care weekend visits, as a result. Most often I was on my own, but sometimes I think my younger brother Larry (named after our father) came along too.

Ironically, these weekend visits were somewhat fun since Mom had passed and we were full-time residents at the orphanage. The visits provided a welcome change of pace.

On various weekends, I was carted from one foster home to the next by a counsellor. It was always the same: I'd stand behind the counsellor as he spoke in hushed tones to the people on the other side of the door. I just wanted to know where I was going, but it felt like I was always on the outside, looking in; a theme that would repeat itself throughout my formative years.

I remember one home in which there was a young son who must have been my age. We played well together and, best of all, we went to a hockey game (it must have been London Knights, though I don't recall) and somehow I ended up with a puck from the game which really made me feel special. I confess, there were some families I went to that I prayed I could have stayed with. Life there was orderly and everyone seemed happy. I was jealous of the kids who were already part of those families.

Why couldn't I have that? I deserved that. I think I would have definitely been adopted in one or more of those homes had it not been for the attempt to keep us six all together. In the end, that wasn't possible, as I'll share shortly.

Following Mom's death, little did I know, my life was about to have a major change that would impact me forever. The challenges that followed forced me to find a new way to survive, if I was ever going to find my true self. To find Stephen Pierson, again.

Chapter 5

OUTSIDE THE DOOR LOOKING IN

July 2, 1974. It's the official date that I went from being Stephen John Henry Pierson to Steven John Henry Barendregt. The adoption order was signed and sealed. I had just turned eleven.

After mom died in May of 1971, we tried to get to some sense of normalcy. At least school was out by June, so we didn't have to worry about that. But I was still lost. I often had nightmares and was confused most of the time. I remember relying heavily on my siblings. Thankfully they were nearby. We were still at the Safe House orphanage. By the end of that summer, we were told that there was a family who owned a big farm and who had taken an interest in us Piersons. I remember the caretakers at the Safe House asking us how we would like to go live on a big farm. The thought was exciting for me. We would all be together. Who wouldn't love that idea, right? Then they mentioned that all of us except our oldest brother Gord would go. *What? How could that even be possible?* I remember there being a lot of chatter about this; not having Gord to come along was just wrong. If I was feeling this way, how were my other siblings feeling? How was Gord feeling?

It was the fall of 1971. Nervous, excited, and mostly sad because Gord wasn't with us, we went along with our counselor to meet our new "parents" on the big farm. As we left the city, I remember looking out the car window. Houses and stores became fewer, fields became more plentiful, and I worried if I would ever find my way back.

It was happening again: that all too familiar situation of visiting another foster home for the weekend. The counselor was at the door speaking with our new "parents." And there I was, *outside the door, looking in.*

Dick and Gwen Barendregt had three of their own children; their eldest son Mike, and daughters Cheryl and Susan. Mike was thirteen years old; the same age as my brother Bill. I came to understand later that the reason they decided not to adopt our eldest brother Gord was because he would have been older than their son Mike. Someone decided that wouldn't be a good idea. They hadn't consulted me, because I hated the idea and was angry about the decision for many years.

Dick Barendregt was a big man; or at least he seemed big to me when I first met him. He had a sheepish smile; almost awkward. He gazed towards me through his wire framed glasses. His eyes were blue and seemingly innocent. He was bald. Not balding but literally had no hair at all. Looking back, I would have thought him much older than his actual age of thirty-five years. He had strong looking arms and muscular forearms; a product of a life lived on the farm. His hands were big and not so soft, likely because they were immersed in soil and earth nearly every day. Gwen was a short person; maybe five foot five. She had dark wavy hair. There was an uneasiness about her that was reflected by my own uneasiness in her company. She too had an awkward smile. Her dark eyes pierced through her dark framed glasses.

The introduction to the Barendregt family was easier on me, I felt, because I had been through this process perhaps more than the others at the various foster care weekends. I remember shaking Mr. Barendregt's hand. I don't think I remembered ever shaking such a big strong hand before. I was proud of myself when he commented at how well I shook his hand. That was something that stayed with me forever. The way I shook everyone's hand from then on was always firm. I taught my own kids the same and said "a firm handshake tells a lot about a person." I always equate a firm handshake as being confident and genuine. I believe this holds true for most, but not always.

Outside the Door Looking In

I confess that the day we were introduced to the Barendregts was a selfish moment for me. I just wanted them to notice me, to like me, to give me a sense of belonging again. I was almost putting myself front and centre at the expense of my siblings. *I wanted them to notice me!*

I especially remember meeting their eldest son Mike for the first time. He had the whitest blond hair; almost glowing. And his front tooth was silver-capped. I had never seen anything like that before. Next in line was their daughter Cheryl who was a couple years older than me and the same age as my sister Susie.

So here is where it got tricky. My sister was always Susie to us. The Barendregt's youngest daughter was also named Susan. Susan was the same age as my youngest brother Larry. Having two girls in the same "family" with the same name presented a problem. There was a solution to this but that wouldn't come until nearly three years later when we were officially adopted. For now, Susie was Susie and Susan was just that.

We moved from the "formal" introductions and headed outside. After all, this was a farm and the six of us had never hung out on a farm before; there was so much to explore. Outside, the first thing I noticed to the side of the house was a row of the biggest pine trees I had ever seen.

I saw a row of boards attached to the trees, stacked one by one on top of each other. *Was it a ladder?* Then, there it was: a tree house.

I remember my smile must have been bigger than my belly. I immediately made my way, my brothers in tow, to climb that tree to the house. I was in heaven, man. Truly, in heaven.

And then, Mike quickly jumped in front of me and declared, "This is MY tree house."

Can you blame him? I mean there he was, a thirteen year old kid, always used to having his own things, his own space. His prized possessions were suddenly being taken over by these kids who weren't even his school friends. We were just a bunch of new kids he didn't even know.

I really can't say what Mike was thinking, but then a few moments later he was gracious enough to take the lead and welcomed us up to the fort.

Later that same day, walking about the farm, I noticed Mike's bike. Man, it was the coolest thing I had ever seen. It had what I remember was a console-like gear shifter and was bright yellow. There I was again, imagining myself on that bike without a thought of it being Mike's.

I don't believe I was jealous of Mike, but I remember thinking that I stood a better chance of having "all these things" living there than if I was living at the orphanage. I was sure of that. The rest of the tour around the farm was uneventful but this was where I would live for the next few years, and I was ok with that.

But we're talking about a farmhouse that would soon house eight children and two parents. Ten people in one household; three of their own children and the five of us Pierson kids. What were they thinking? Had they thought this out? Those questions would come up again years later for me. But for now, I was content.

Since it was fall, school was on the agenda. I was excited to see our new school. I would be in grade three. One afternoon, we all piled into the station wagon and Dick drove us to see Sparta-Union Public School.

I remember the drive vividly because Dick's mother, Celia Barendregt, came for the drive with us too. Celia would become Gramma Barendregt to me. She had lost her husband, Klaas about eight years prior to us coming into the Barendregt family. He was only sixty-four years of age. Celia was only fifty-one when he died. She never remarried despite her being such a young widow. I never met Klaas, of course, but I heard many stories about him over the years. All of them were about his good nature and his hard work. Everyone spoke of his integrity. I wish I had known him. I expect we would have gotten along quite well.

In contrast to the stiffness of my new parents, Gramma Barendregt was a kinder soul. She had an infectious laugh and an affectionate smile. You know, the smile that shows the love a person feels when directed at you.

Her eyes were the type that allowed you to catch a glimpse of her soul at times. I could see her heartache at the loss of her husband on one hand, and then you would catch a glimpse of her mischievous nature. I felt an immediate connection to her. I knew rather quickly I could rely on her for comfort and guidance.

As the years passed, this inkling I had of her would prove to be very true. She would become a major and positive influence in my life until the day she died.

I remember the first time I saw our new school. They had a playground and a field out back that seemed to go on forever. To me the school looked modern, and I couldn't wait to get started.

We were told that we would go to school everyday by school bus. This was new to all of us Pierson kids. This would be another environment in which I would have to reintroduce myself to new people. But I was ready. On the drive home from school, I remember my youngest brother Larry, who would have been six years old at this point, got into an argument with our older brother Bill. I don't remember what they were arguing about but I will never forget Larry telling Bill to "fuck off."

Dick must have hammered hard on the brakes, because the car came to a jolting halt. I think he must have been furious because his face was red and if I wasn't exaggerating, he had fire in his eyes.

"Who just said that?"

The car went quiet. But to us Pierson kids, that vocabulary was normal. I really didn't think much of it at that moment. Obviously, Dick (and I'm certain Celia as well) was in total shock, hearing that coming from the mouth of a six year old. The rest of the drive back home was completely quiet. That wouldn't be the last time I witnessed the wrath of Dick Barendregt's anger.

Those being the early months living with the Barendregt's on the farm, we had occasional visits from our counselor at the Children's Aid

Society. No doubt, Dick and Gwen Barendregt had to decide whether this new arrangement would work before there was any final decision on adoption.

During these visits, I remember being asked by the counselor how everything was going. These questions were never asked of us discreetly, so the answer was always the same; *great!* To be fair, at this time it was great. For the first time in my life, I felt a sense of stability. A sense of uninterrupted security; if only for a while.

The neat thing about the school bus was that I got to meet many new friends. These friends were the same kids on my bus route and it allowed us all to bond in a way that couldn't be done during class time. Day in and day out, riding that bus together allowed us to share stories and plan our lives around those drives together.

My grade three teacher was Mrs. Lang. I remember I liked her. I didn't know it at the time, but she was well aware of our story; living in the community and knowing about the Barendregt family that had adopted us. I mentioned earlier that my math skills were not the best, having been in and out of so many schools throughout grades one and two. But I was very good at reading and spelling.

Mrs. Lang always asked me to read, and she always praised me for my reading skills. It's still fascinating to me that her encouragement was one of my first memories of positive reinforcement. I loved the attention and I did whatever I had to do to keep on the receiving end of her praise. I was always seeking attention because I had lacked it since my mom's death. It wasn't the same kind of attention I'd receive from Dick when I reached grade four and he took issue with my math skills, or lack thereof.

Fortunately, I sought attention in positive ways like being a good reader, or by doing good deeds. I wasn't stealing or doing bad deeds. Despite my best efforts, however, I was largely ignored by my new parents; especially by Gwen, from whom I craved even a little doting, as the female head of the household. Because of the lack of love and affection,

I learned to seek it through others. It would be positive reinforcement that would shape me for years to come.

Here's a funny story: One day, in grade three, we were asked to write our names on a form. I paused and, somewhat embarrassed, I asked Mrs. Lang to come to my desk. I explained that I didn't know how to spell "Barendregt." Even though I wasn't officially adopted yet, it was important to me to fit in. I wanted to use the Barendregt name. She smiled and wrote it out for me. I proceeded to proudly submit my new name: *Steven John Henry Barendregt.*

I remember having a big smile when I went to hand it to Mrs. Lang. I headed back to my desk and I heard, "Steven, you're funny."

I turned and asked why. She said, "When I asked for your 'John Henry,' I didn't expect you to actually write it."

What was she saying to me? What had I done wrong? She explained to me that the term, "Write your John Henry" was a request to sign your name. I still didn't really get the humour but when I told her that was indeed my full name, she smiled and let me sit down.

Chapter 6

ADOPTED AGAIN?

One day at recess, this reddish blonde-haired kid with freckles approached me. He was one of my fellow school bus mates and a student in my grade three class.

"Hey, do you wanna be friends? My name is Ken Pfeffer."

At that time I was having some difficulty fitting in, so of course I said yes. I didn't give it another thought, really.

I remember having a best friend when my mom was alive. His name was Dale Pettit. He lived across the street from me on Dufferin Ave. I never saw him again after Mom died. I had hoped Ken would become my new best friend; someone I could share my secrets with, a confidant. We hit it off well because I think we were opposites. I was much more outgoing and he was quieter. Pairing up with Ken that day was one of the wisest personal choices I have ever made.

Being with the Pfeffer clan was an escape for me: life with the Barendregts was becoming more tense. We kids were still adjusting to our "new normal." I know I was still hurting from the loss of Mom; and no doubt my siblings were too. I was still confused with many of the new changes living in this new family. I still remember just wanting to be loved and held again; like Mom used to do.

Once, when I was about eight years of age, I was crying about something and just wanted some reassurance - a hug. I reached up to Gwen Barendregt for that hug. It didn't come. In fact, as long as I remember to this day, my adopted mother never hugged me once.

Even at a young age at the Barendregt's, nearly every weekend was a work weekend. I learned quickly on a Saturday mornings to find something to do or Dick would find something for me to do. This would often be a task that was much harder than what I'd come up with.

As often as I could, I would "escape" by pre-planning a stay-over with my pal Ken. His family lived about ten concessions from me.

A "concession line" is principally an Ontario term for the straight country roads, parallel to one another, upon which farm lots face.

The Pfeffers were not farmers, although Ken's Grandparents, who lived just down from their home, had a farm that they didn't tend to. What Ken did have though, was a tree fort that he was more than happy to share with me. We spent hours in that fort. It was a place where we shared many stories, laughed and planned our lives. It was my freedom from the stress that was building at home for me.

Ken had four siblings. His brother Johnny was the oldest. He also had three sisters: Darlene and Joy were older than Ken, while Diane was the youngest. The house was a white picket fenced home, with one bathroom and shared bedrooms; one for all three girls and one that Ken and Johnny shared. Johnny was older than us by five or six years and by the time I was staying overnight, John was never around much. This left the bedroom for just me and Ken.

What Johnny did leave behind under the mattress, was his collection of "girlie" magazines. Finding those was like hitting the jackpot for two growing boys! Those magazines found their way to the fort and along with us on many camping trips we shared over the years.

Because Ken remains my best friend today, I know that the Pfeffer home is still occupied by Ken's mom. I have such fond memories of that home. Even listening to the three girls scream over some argument was music to my ears, because I felt safe there.

Adopted Again?

Outside the bedrooms was a living room with a couch, two lounge chairs and a single TV. The kitchen was the largest room in the house. This made a lot of sense because we spent so much time around the large table as a family. The kitchen made the home, that's for sure. My memory stretches long and wide of eating some of the best meals there, complete with homemade pies and generous portions of ice cream. Mother Pfeffer always had a candy dish full of chocolates and candies which was never found at the Barendregt household. I took advantage of the candy dish many times.

Many evenings after dinner, we would play games around the table. Playing "spoons" was dangerous. As an adult, I recall Joy and I charging to grab the spoon to avoid losing and her nails darn near ripped my arm apart.

On another overnight stay at the Pfeffer's, I decided to sleep on the couch in the living room. I believe it was a "new" used couch. When I woke up I was covered in a red rash everywhere. I had no idea what had happened but I sure was itchy. Mother Pfeffer laughed and laughed. It turned out the couch was full of fleas.

Ken's parents, Jack and Joyce, welcomed me into their family as if I was one of their own, from Day One. I remember telling Joyce that my mom's name was also Joyce. What was more, they had birthdays that were exactly thirteen days apart. Ken's mom confided in me that she was meant to have six children, but her first child had died. Even at that young age, I was formulating an understanding, making sense as to why we must have met for a reason. It made me feel good. It made me feel like this was meant to be. I belonged there.

At that time, I asked myself if I'd been adopted into the wrong family. This thinking was reinforced when I learned that Ken's dad's legal name was actually John Henry Pfeffer. There it was; I knew it: MY name was Steven JOHN HENRY too!

I secretly decided that I belonged there. It was a sign from heaven. I mean, why not? My mom was giving me a sign. Everything made sense to me. I was the child that Joyce lost and now I was found. Whether I was right or wrong, it didn't matter. I was content to live secretly thinking this, and this combination of unexplained happenstance and collected coincidences helped me feel a sense of true belonging.

As the years went by, Ken and I often found ourselves in the same elementary class. And when we weren't, recesses and lunches provided an opportunity to hook up and play. We joined Cub Scouts and then Scouts together. Scouts, in particular, was where we both excelled and discovered our love for camping.

I was spending so much time with the Pfeffer's, I think even some of the locals began wondering if I hadn't been adopted by them. I was so comfortable at this point that I was even calling Joyce *Mother*. Ken's dad, Jack, was more reserved, and I never built-up the nerve to call him Dad until many years later. Mother was my strongest supporter at that age. Anytime I felt the need for love and attention, I just had to go to Ken's place and receive it.

Mother knew how much Ken and I loved to go camping. She herself parked a camper every summer at a local camping site near home; she loved camping too. I spent many times there with her and Ken and the rest of the gang. I learned to fish because of Ken and Mother. These days, when I'm fishing alone, I often find myself wondering back to those first memories of fishing with Ken and Mother at the camping park in Catfish Creek. This was perhaps the beginning of my love affair with nature.

Living where we did, there were lots of places to camp with woods and streams. Fortunately, the Barendregt's owned many acres of land. One of the farms they owned was along the lake bank of Lake Erie; near Port Stanley. It had a fast running stream and a beautiful wooded area. The property was labeled *Hawk Cliff* because of the migration of hawks there every fall. Today, Hawk Cliff is recognized as one of the best places in North America from which to observe the fall hawk migration.

By the time I reached the age of thirteen, I was expected to work on the farm even more during summer. This hampered our ability to go camping like we used to. Therefore, Ken and I decided we could still camp during March break. Yes, it was a lot colder and even snowier, but it was a chance to get away while the farm chores were less demanding. Mother Pfeffer would always help us plan the trip. She never blinked an eye when we asked her for what seemed to be everything but the kitchen sink to bring with us. I still hear her laughing; see her beautiful big smile as she marvelled at us planning. I loved her then as I love her now.

With all our gear loaded up in her car, she would drive us to the farm where we portaged into the woods. But Mother wouldn't just drop us off. No, that was not her style. I think she had as much fun grabbing whatever we couldn't carry in several trips and hiking back in with us; laughing all the way. Depending on where we stepped in the snow, someone would inevitably break through and fill their boots with water. Mother would laugh and laugh.

Maybe it was just so she knew where we would be staying those few days during March Break, but I really think she was just supporting our dreams. She always did and still does. She paid for all the food, all the snacks, and I think the only thing she didn't pay for were the infamous girlie magazines that we scooped from Johnny's mattress. I'm sure she knew about our stash, but she never said a word.

Using our Scouts' training, Ken and I would set up elaborate camping sites. This became an annual trek that we looked forward to every March Break. We added my brothers, Dan and Larry, as well as other school chums on our various journeys into the woods. We took pride in building a better campsite every year. Depending on how many we had in the camp, we would have one to two tents set up for lodging and a separate tent for the food. We would break smaller tree limbs in about two to three foot lengths and place them end to end; making an above-the-snow walking path from one tent to the other. This allowed us to walk between tents without our heavy and often muddy boots.

Setting-up camp was always memorable. Ken was by far the best organized. He would get so cranky because of our inability in setting up the tents. I'd be standing there freezing cold and shivering while Ken would be sweating profusely. I would be amazed how he could be sweating while I was so cold. Obviously, he was the one moving and getting things done and I was not. Before long, we would get to the set-up of the focal point: the fire. We had so many stories and fun around those fires. All throughout high school, we made it a point of keeping these trips up. I believe those camping trips defined who we were and who we would become. Even after high school, I remained a fixture within the Pfeffer clan.

Chapter 7

IN CHAOS, I FIND MY CENTRE

When I was about ten, we'd been living with the Barendregts' for about two years. It was around this time I remember being told we were moving.

Oh my God, I thought. We're moving again?

It took me back to my orphanage days; all the moving around. I felt sick.

When I realized that the move was just up the road and everything including our school was the same, I felt better. It became obvious that ten people needed more room. We moved into what I learned was "the home farm." This was Dick's parents' farm, where he grew up. Celia Barendregt, Dick's mom, whom I will refer to as Gramma B still lived in the home farm house with her youngest son, John Barendregt. John was soon-to-be married and would need a place of his own. I believe the events unfolded like this: A new bungalow home across the road from the home farm would be built for Gramma B. John and his new bride, Valerie, would move into the farmhouse where we were. Dick, Gwen, and all of us kids would move into the larger home farm house.

Obviously with eight kids; five boys and three girls, renovations would be needed. All the kids' bedrooms were upstairs while Dick and Gwen's bedroom was on the main floor. With the renovations, the upstairs was split between the boys' side and the girl's side. Oddly, this was similar to the orphanage we left. The girls' half of the upstairs was at the rear of the house and the boys', at the front. There was one bathroom for all eight of us, but at least we had double sinks. Anyone seeing this layout for the first time would have thought they stumbled upon the seven dwarfs movie set. There were five boy's beds all in a row; no walls. What a sight that was. Across the other side, my sister Susie and Cheryl shared a large bedroom. Susan, the youngest, had her own room near the bathroom.

When privacy walls were finally added on the boys' side, we were short one brother. Bill had run away back to London. Dan and I shared a room on the west side that overlooked the flower garden and field. Although I hated losing another brother, I liked my new room.

Dan was an awesome roommate. He loved rock and roll music and was much more artistic and talented in that way than I was. He even taught himself to play guitar. He had all the records that were cool. We played them low in the evening as we went off to bed. I remember so many of those songs when I hear them today, and they remind me of brother Dan. One bedroom, in the middle, with a big window was for our youngest brother Larry, and the East side of the front of the house was Mike's room.

By 1974, we were pretty settled into our new life. By July, we were officially adopted as Barendregt's. We still had two "Susan's" in the family; my older sister "Sue" and the youngest daughter of Dick and Gwen, Susan.

Through the adoption process, a legal name change was possible. I thought this may be fun. *Wow! What would I change my name to?*

I remember thinking up some "cool" names. I remember asking to change my middle name from John Henry to something else. I'll give Gwen credit for explaining to me that I was probably named after a special relative of mine. Years later, I learned my middle name was indeed named after my biological grandfather John Henry Pierson. She convinced me to keep that name and I am grateful to her for that.

During this time we were calling my sister "Sue" and the youngest of the Barendregt kids, "Susan." Changing her name was not as much fun for her. She exclaimed several times how she wanted to keep her own name. She had stated this was all she had left to hang on to our mother.

Back then, it never dawned on me as much as it did in my later years just how difficult this was for her. But Dick and Gwen made it very clear: Susan Pierson had to change her name from Sue because their daughter was already Susan. Her entire life my sister was known as Susie when younger and Sue when she was older. When we started our new school in 1971 coming to the Barendregt's, Sue was in grade five. She was known as Sue Pierson from grade five through seven. In the fall of 1974, Sue Pierson began grade eight and had to explain to all who knew her. She was no longer Sue Pierson but was now "Sandi Barendregt." Talk about losing your identity. It must have been hard for such a young girl coming into her own at that age. Sandi resented the name change for a long time and I don't blame her. At least by the time she started high school, only those who knew her before would know the difference. The bulk of her new friends would only know her as Sandi Barendregt from then on.

We were all making adjustments; so many of us under one roof. I know us Pierson kids were struggling to adhere to so many new rules. By now, we were officially calling Dick and Gwen; Mom and Dad, but something was still wrong. We were still two "camps" living in the same house. Dick and Gwen still referred to us Pierson kids as "you Pierson kids," especially if we did something wrong. They made us all feel like there was something wrong with being a Pierson. I was accepting of not being called a Pierson, but when it was used, it was frequently used in a demoralizing way that made me feel small.

By fall, I was entering grade five. Something new in our household; high school. Bill and Mike were starting high school. Based on where we lived, kids from our rural area were supposed to attend the high school closer to the farm. That was Parkside Collegiate, located outside of the city limits. Parkside was a newer high school. However, the high school that Dick Barendregt attended was Arthur Voaden Secondary School

(AVSS), located in the small town of St. Thomas, Ontario. It was decided that the boys would attend AVSS.

Brother Bill was a stocky guy in comparison to his classmates. It was no surprise that he was asked to play football in his junior year. AVSS had a history of winning more football titles than not. One of the coaches named Mr. (Al) Youngash recruited Bill. This must have been a real confidence booster for him. I think this could have been a turning point for Bill. He, like the rest of us Pierson kids, was still feeling down and out of place.

It's not uncommon for adopted children to have many different feelings as a result of being adopted. We may often feel rejected, abandoned, guilty and disconnected. During adolescence, we often search for self identity. Many who are adopted at, or near, birth who don't know their birth parents, experience feelings of being disloyal when they seek to find their biological parents. With us Pierson kids, we knew who our parents were. The lack of having a real relationship with either of them, however, created problems for me as I grew older.

I developed a feeling of abandonment. When I started developing relationships; particularly with the opposite sex, my feeling of being abandoned manifested into an unhealthy sense of jealousy, doubt and lack of trust. Living with Dick and Gwen certainly did nothing to diminish our feeling of being disconnected. Even after we were officially adopted, they continued to label us as "The Pierson kids," especially if we did something wrong. It was always "you Piersons" or "that's the Pierson blood in you."

I can only trust that the governmental agencies do more to ensure adopting parents are better trained to recognize that adopted children need extra care and attention to help them with predisposed feelings.

I dealt with my attempt to nurture my own self identity by being outgoing. I was comfortable talking to anyone. I was always seeking attention and approval of others. I was able to control this by being outgoing. I was happy to learn what someone needed and solve it for them. In the truest sense, I was a pleaser. One thing I learned much later in my life was that by being a pleaser, you are often taken advantage of by others. I have learned the subtle difference between being a pleaser and genuine kindness. The latter is entirely selfless while the other may be pathological in nature.

In both cases, not dealing with abandonment and self identity issues affected my relationships and ultimately led to two unhappy marriages. The great thing about growing older, is that we have the opportunity to perfect our weaknesses and in so doing, improve our lives as well as the lives of others around us.

Neither Dick or Gwen really went out of their way to recognize the help and the nurturing we Pierson kids needed. Perhaps it was because Bill was going to be headed to high school that Dick and Gwen were particularly hard on him. But why Bill and not Mike? Of course, this was no fault of Mike's but us Pierson kids were sure getting used to being subjected to a different set of rules and punishments that were much harsher than those lavished on their biological kids.

At night, or wherever we knew we were not within earshot, Bill, Dan and I would discuss together how bad things seemed to be. Bill started talking about running away. That scared me.

Bill joined the football team and proved Coach Youngash right. Bill ended-up being a superstar defensive tackle. Already in his first year, he was making a name for himself. Football was a release from the tension Bill had at home. He confided in me later in life that football was the only thing that kept him from losing it altogether. It didn't strike me back then, but when I reflect upon it now, I can't help but feel how things might have been different.

Why wouldn't Dick and Gwen take an interest and celebrate Bill's newfound success in football? Why didn't they take the time to encourage him, to nurture this talent? Why wouldn't they just come to a game and watch him and cheer him on? Build his confidence through positive reinforcement? The high school was about 15 kilometers from the farm. By foot, it would take an hour and a half. In order for Bill to play football, that was the condition; that he walk home everyday after practice. Why? By car it would have taken no more than fifteen minutes. But that never happened. Bill was building his anger every step of the way home. He was planning his "escape" from the Barendregt's.

Dick's youngest brother was John, who was quite a bit younger than him. John and his new wife Valerie were now living in the farmhouse we vacated earlier. I remember Uncle John and Aunt Valerie took a liking to Bill. Frankly, they treated all of us kids with love and kindness; in my opinion, more so than did Dick and Gwen. Uncle John offered to step-in and try to help; take "Billy" under his wing and nurture him a bit. Dad would have nothing to do with it. So things just got worse and more tense.

Dad was pretty strict and had little patience. Talking back or anything of the sort was not tolerated. Resorting to physical violence was normal. We were growing accustomed to his yelling and physical abuse. It was a terrible feeling. We were always on edge and didn't know what may happen if we ever stepped out of line.

You remember I stated earlier to be sure you had a job on Saturday or Dick would find you one? One day, all of us Pierson boys (Bill, Dan, Larry, and I) were in the barn shop. At least it was a little warm in the barn as we swept, cleaned, and organized. I'm not certain who was arguing, but Dick heard us and he came in. He had that fire in his eyes that I had seen before. He was yelling and kicked us all out of the shop into the cold day. Bill grunted a quiet "fuck-off" under his breath but loud enough that Dick heard it. I was already outside the shop door when BOOM! As I turned, I saw Bill flying through the air as Dick had kicked him so hard that he "flew" out the door.

I was feeling like I had felt years before; standing on the front lawn watching mom and dad fighting with all the neighbours lined along the street as if they were watching the main event of some boxing match. "I deserve better; we all deserved better," I thought.

How did we end-up here? Even in the foster care homes I went to, I didn't feel this afraid. Even as irresponsible as our old man was, I don't think I ever felt as afraid and lonely as I was living in this environment with Dick and Gwen. We were literally walking on eggshells.

Clearly, that was a turning point for Bill. I remember a few nights later he came to me and Dan and told us he was running away. He planned to go back to London where he would stay with our older brother Gord.

I was afraid for Bill. I was afraid for all of us. With Bill gone, who would protect us? What would Dick do when he found out? Oh my God; he will surely kill him. Then, one day Bill never came home from highschool. He was gone. This would draw Dan and I even closer. Twelve year-old Dan was now my protector.

Once Bill was gone, there was little talk about his leaving. I think it would have benefitted us younger kids to have talked openly about this with Dick and Gwen but why would they? They had not shown any love and compassion since the beginning and they sure weren't interested in admitting that maybe they could have done better. This must have added pressure on Dan because he knew both Larry and I were relying on him now.

Our older sister Sandi was somewhat spared from the physical abuse from Dick, but I often wondered how she dealt with having Gwen as her "role model." I imagine that Sandi needed a mother-daughter relationship, but never got one. I always felt that Sandi was able to overcome the challenges of being a "Pierson" while in the Barendregt home. Knowing her today, she has tougher skin than most and adapts to any environment; good or bad. I won't even begin to speak for her feelings as we were growing up because I know there were hardships for her too. In fact, I recall she too ran away from home one day. She was about 16 years old and was active in figure skating. She came home from skating and was in a rush to get to her studies because she had an exam the next morning. She hung her coat up on the coat rack and ran upstairs.

In a few minutes we could all hear Gwen yelling as if something was seriously wrong.

"Sandi, you get down here this minute!"

Apparently, Sandi had hung her coat up on the wrong hook. Gwen called Sandi out on this infraction and proceeded to punch her in the face, causing her nose to bleed. I remember hearing Sandi cry. She too was now screaming.

I had learned to keep my mouth shut; all of us did, otherwise we'd suffer the same wrath.

How crazy our world seemed to be getting.

Why was the careless placement of a coat such an issue? Surely, it wasn't cause for concern; much less a beating. Alarmingly, this was becoming the norm in our household.

Sandi ran down the road to a family we knew well. The Verbruggen family lived on a concession South of the farm. Sandi knew Diane and John Verbruggen well since she often babysat for them. She hid out there and I remember she was adamant she would never come back. It wouldn't be the last time John and Diane Verbruggen helped us Pierson kids out. Sandi eventually came home later that evening.

Again, nothing much was said about it. Another opportunity for Dick and Gwen to assess what the hell was going wrong and where things could be improved. I think because Sandi and I were a lot alike, we didn't seem to get along very well when I was aged ten to twelve. I can't say it was really bad but there was the normal sibling rivalry. I was likely always bugging her about adolescent issues as she was growing into a young woman and getting ready for bigger and better things in high school. By the time I reached age thirteen, Sandi and I rekindled our previously strong sister-brother bond. I remember feeling so happy when we found common ground. We have remained close siblings ever since and I am happier for it.

Cheryl was Dick and Gwen's second child. Cheryl and Sandi were the same age and I think, as best as I remember, they got along pretty well. I don't recall many arguments although you would expect that not to be the case as they grew older. Cheryl was a pretty girl and I remember her fondly growing up. She was also quite smart in school and I envied her for that.

Cheryl probably got herself into more trouble because of us Pierson siblings than she would have if left to her own devices. To this day, she is an advocate for righting a wrong or fighting for the underdog. I know Cheryl saw the injustice being done when it came to the "Pierson" kids; particularly us remaining boys. She defended us against both Dick and Gwen countless times and I loved her for it. Without Cheryl pleading our case to the parents, I'm sure we would have been physically or emotionally abused even more than we were.

When I was eighteen or nineteen years old, Cheryl was at the right place at the right time; she literally saved me from taking my own life. I was in a bad place, having failed out of my second semester of college. I had a menial job. I had little money to do what I wanted to do. I had lost my way. Normally, I was the eternal optimist, but things just piled up at that point in my life. I had just finished spending Thanksgiving weekend by myself, in my car. I was feeling sorry for myself. For the first time in my life, I didn't feel like I deserved better. You might say that my spark was nearly extinguished. I was headed to the lake bank to drive my car off of it. I had been there many times before as the land was owned by Dick.

Cheryl's family home was just at the intersection of the main road and the road to the lake bank. As I approached the corner to head down the road, Cheryl was working in her yard and she saw my car. She waved and I was compelled to stop. She simply said, "And what are you doing, Steve?" I took a deep breath-in, welled up and replied, "I was going to drive my car over the lake bank." Her eyes softened and she quietly whispered, "I think you better come in for a coffee so we can chat; give me your keys." I'm grateful for her being there that day. She was the vessel that the universe provided for me that day.

Though Cheryl and I don't see each other much at all anymore, it's not because we're angry at one another. We had, years before, spent time around a campfire at the cottage. We would talk about the "old days," but I think the past haunts us both enough to stay apart; I don't know.

One thing I've come to realize is as much as it was difficult for me and my adopted siblings, it was difficult for the three Barendregt kids too. They didn't ask for the life that Dick and Gwen chose for them either. Their otherwise "normal" family life was completely turned upside down when the Pierson kids arrived. They lost whatever sense of normalcy they once had. Adults consulting with young children over adult issues is unfair. Dick and Gwen should have known the implications of bringing a whole new family into the home. It was no different when the case worker from the CAS asked me, "How is everything at the Barendregt's going?" with Dick and Gwen standing in the same room. What else was I going to answer? "It's fine, just fine." I have found peace and reconciliation in the understanding that Mike, Cheryl and Susan being the biological Barendregt kids were as much victims as us Pierson kids. I didn't see that as an adolescent.

As Sandi and Cheryl went off to high school, Dan and I were in grade seven and eight together. Dan had stepped back a grade. We were both average students but what Dan had over me was his athleticism. He was a natural at anything to do with sports; and in elementary school, that was gym class and track and field. Dan could run like the wind. It was nothing for him to win several ribbons at track and field. In gym class, he could scale a rope at lightning speed.

Being set back a grade, Dan, of course, was a year older; and combined with his super star athletic ability, how could I compete with that? I was never jealous of that reality because I still looked up to him, so all seemed right with the world in that regard. I was so proud of Dan at grade eight graduation when he was awarded the "Most Improved" student award. It validated the heartbreak I know he felt when he stepped back a year.

As is so important for each of us, I eventually found my "thing." I started public speaking in grade school. In grade four, it was mandatory that we write a speech and deliver it to the class. So many of my classmates were terrified of this, but I wasn't at all. I felt a natural "high" about the prospects of speaking in front of the class.

I'd remembered from grade three how I was praised for how well I read aloud. No track and field ribbons were in my future but what about a trophy for speaking?

The time came when I had to deliver my speech. I had butterflies, but they weren't because of having to read my speech. These butterflies were the result of finding out whether or not I'd be picked to read in the gymnasium. You see, only those who were good enough would be selected to present to the entire school.

I did well, but I didn't win the class event. I was let down but was even more determined to try again. It was at this stage in my life that I developed a keen sense of competition. I was beginning to understand my strengths. If not as an athlete, then as a speaker.

Every year that went by, I was ready to write a new speech. By grade six, I was developing well as an orator and each year my confidence grew. Even by losing, I felt I was winning.

At that time, I entered the annual Optimist Club Oratorical contest. This would bring the best of the best orators to compete. I had an ace in the hole, I like to say. Gramma Barendregt, "Gramma B" lived across the road from us. I loved her dearly, and she always had time for me and instilled confidence in me - something that I shared with her in my later years.

Everyday, when I got off the school bus, I made it my "chore" to get the mail from her mailbox and deliver it to her. It gave me the opportunity to share my day with her. She always listened intently. When I told her about my oratorical contest that year, she insisted on helping me.

This became a ritual. After dropping off her mail, I would grab a homemade cookie and then head to her living room. She taught me to stand tall and be sure to look up as often as I could to make it like I knew every word of my speech. She taught me to read slowly and clearly. She would make sure I knew and understood the difficult words I had used in my speech. Under Gramma B's tutelage, I honed my skills. We kept up this tradition until I stopped entering speaking contests.

I realized, years later, that she was doing a lot more for me than speech writing and oration. She was making me a better person. She was building my confidence and helping me to forget the challenges going on across the road at the home farm. I know she knew far more than she ever let on about what was happening across the road. But, I'm guessing, for valid reasons, she stayed quiet. This was her way of helping silently. I adored this woman and helped her with any chore I could think of from weeding gardens and cutting lawns, to shoveling snow. I just felt safe around her.

One day, I delivered her mail as usual. Gramma had just baked homemade cookies again. She asked me if I wanted to sit down and have one with a glass of milk. Who wouldn't? It was speech night for me and so we ran through the script one last time before I was set to deliver that evening. We talked and talked and I ate more cookies than I should have.

I headed across the road for home. Gwen was waiting for me at the door when I came in. She said, "And where have you been, Mister?"

Surprisingly, I said, "At Gramma's, like I always am after school."

I knew Gwen was in a foul mood as she retorted, "Don't you smart mouth me." Then she punched me right in the face.

I was dazed as she punched me again and said "YOU young man had better be ready for when Dad comes home after THAT smart mouth. Don't you ever mouth me back again."

This was becoming normal for me. All too often, Gwen would go out of her way to bring another incident up to Dick for disciplinary action. Some days I could even see Dick not wanting to deal with another incident Gwen raised. I suppose to keep peace with his wife, he went along with the charade; playing judge, jury and executioner.

That particular evening was a double-whammy for me. It was report card night at the supper table on the very same night I had to compete in the oratorical contest. Report cards for me were often a problem. My marks were always fine, but the dreaded teacher's remarks always included, "*Steven is talkative in class.*"

I knew better. I knew this was a problem for Dick and yet every year it was the same. I couldn't help myself. I was a social butterfly and often bored when my work was done. I was seeking attention. I'm not sure what all the fuss was about, but Dick despised it.

So I had to be at the Optimist Club for 7 PM. It was about 5:30 PM at the dinner table. I had already been smacked around earlier by Gwen. Dick started going through the report cards and my stomach was churning. I was bracing for what may come.

And then it happened. Dick read it aloud: "Steven is talkative in class."

So picture our kitchen table: four kids on each side and the parents at each end; so a long table. I sat to Dick's right side, second from the end. I barely saw it coming, but I felt it hit my chin after bouncing off the table in front of me. Dick hurled his glass mug at me. You know those heavy old style root beer mugs? My heart was pounding and my chin bleeding. I dared not move. I was stunned and felt sick.

Once I gathered myself, I just sat there and waited for the instruction to get the belt for a strap from him, but it didn't come this time. I announced that perhaps I best not go and give my speech tonight.

He looked up at me and said, "Oh, you have your speech tonight? Well, you'd better get up and get ready."

Shaking like a leaf, I changed from my clothes into a suit and was told Dick was waiting in the car outside. I kept my head down and quietly walked out to the car. Dick drove me to the Optimist club where I would deliver my speech.

It was a very silent drive; neither of us spoke a word. I was merely avoiding any contact with him for fear he would rattle me even more. I was already wondering how I was even going to compose myself. I had a band aid on my chin.

"I look like an idiot," I thought.

Dick dropped me off, per usual. Neither Dick or Gwen ever stayed to watch, or even encourage me.

"Why not?" I always wondered.

But I do remember composing myself well enough to present my speech. Needless to say, I only came in third place and received the bronze trophy that night. All was not lost though. That night I learned a good lesson. I learned to overcome fear and the bullying tactics handed out by my captors (Dick and Gwen). Something came over me like a wave. I developed a sense of confidence that night; transforming me into who I am today.

At the end of the evening, all the contestants were invited to introduce their parents. Of course, I was the only contestant whose parents were not there. With my newfound confidence, I quickly adapted to this challenge. In the crowd was our school principal, Mr. (Angus) Walton. Yes! I would use him to avoid the embarrassment of being the kid whose parents didn't have the sense to be there. I could tell by the order of where I was in the line that my turn was coming up after the two people next to me finished. And then, they called me.

With all the confidence in the world I stepped forward and said, "My parents were unable to attend this evening (*ha ha, they never attended*) but I would now like to take this opportunity to recognize and thank Mr. Walton, our school principal."

Mr. Walton smiled a beautiful big smile and I continued, "For providing me a learning opportunity and helping me grow as a person." I'm sure I saw a tear in his eye, and the thunder of clapping was validation enough for me. Had I been quick enough to add that to my speech that night, I may have won second place at least.

Suddenly, my chin didn't hurt; I was no longer shaking from the fear of Dick and I had an entirely new level of confidence. I knew I would do better next year and I was going to prove it to Dick and Gwen out of spite.

This would be a new adaptive characteristic I used in the coming years that pushed me through so many more challenges living in that house of chaos. But, it worked for me and that was what I needed at the time. Whatever Dick or Gwen said I couldn't do (which was almost everything), I grew stronger and proved them wrong, every time. It became a game that I played. A game I liked, because I was winning.

It seemed to me that I was being challenged on so many levels at this stage of my life and so from age eleven until at least high school I had to test my theory on being confident, proving Dick and Gwen wrong at every chance and just trying to survive.

I remember a few major incidents that happened to me over the next few years. These would test my theory of rising above the chaos and feeling like I had won another battle over Dick and Gwen by surviving whatever they threw my way.

One in particular was when I was forced to sleep in the bathtub for a week. Apparently I was breathing (not snoring) too loudly during my slumber; keeping others awake. Dick and Gwen decided it would be a good idea that I "learn a lesson in how to breathe properly" and made me sleep in their downstairs bathroom. I was given a pillow and a blanket. The tub was cold, not to mention hard. I figured I was at least warmer by putting the blanket underneath me as opposed to on top of me. I asked for an extra blanket but I was told "one was not available."

I laughed inside. I grew stronger inside. I was not going to give them the satisfaction of crying, even though I wanted to. Somehow, I took the high road, again, and made this a game. I pretended that I was a prisoner, wrongfully accused and imprisoned. I think Dick and Gwen figured I could never last, but I did. In fact, I think I ended up in that tub a few days longer than I may have, had I had cried. I would not give them the satisfaction. Through this, I proved I was resilient; another characteristic that has helped me in my personal growth over the years.

Oddly, I developed an ability to breathe very low while sleeping. Even to this day, my wife checks on me from time to time whenever she doesn't hear me breathing. I am certain this was not the intention of Dick and Gwen back then.

There were other instances of neglect and abuse along the way, but I won't list them all. Suffice to say, I was constantly being accused of something.

Being wrongfully accused is a terrible thing. In Dick's world, as a Pierson, you were guilty until he proved otherwise. In grade school we had lunch monitors who were the older kids in school. One of those kids was a young lady whose parents rented a farmhouse at the time from Dick, and so I knew her. During lunch there was some sort of commotion and the young lady was handing out detentions or some form of demerit.

A voice behind me; one of my classmates shouted out, "You're a slut."

I couldn't catch a break at that time. So, the class monitor looked at me and said, "Steven Barendregt, I am telling your dad."

I implored her that I did not say it but, of course, wouldn't tell her who did. I knew I was in trouble if she called, so when I got home, I was anxiously waiting for that phone to ring. It hadn't rang and at 7 PM I thought, ok, she had thought about it and won't bother. I went about my business and then it rang. *Oh God! Was it her?*

I waited, and then suddenly, "STEVE, GET YOUR ASS DOWN HERE RIGHT NOW."

I already knew what it was about. I pleaded it was a misunderstanding and I even told Dick who the guilty party was; after all, I figured it wouldn't matter now. He would hear nothing of it. What he decided to do was one of the most degrading acts a parent could ever do to their child. It still makes me embarrassed (for him) to write about it.

In the morning, Dick called me downstairs before school. He asked Gwen for her eyeliner pencil. She handed it to him and I swear she had a smile on her face. He decided that if I had a foul mouth then I would have to let everyone in the world know. He grabbed my head, told me to close my mouth. Pressing my lips together, he proceeded to use the black eyeliner and wrote across my entire mouth the word **"FILTH."**

He threatened me: "If you wash this off at any time during school, I will kill you."

Imagine, walking the long laneway out of the house to the bus stop. I was already developing a plan of what to say to my friends when they first saw me.

I boarded the bus. The bus driver was a stern man and nothing ever phased him, or so I thought. I could immediately tell from his eyes when he saw me, that even he was in shock.

"Do you need to wash up, Steve?" he asked.

I remember saying "No, Mr. Somerville, I'm actually trying an experiment today."

I proceeded to the back of the bus. Of course, whispers, jeers, and shock from everyone, as I expected. What was I supposed to do? I was going to be killed if I dared take it off. I sunk down into my seat as low as I could to hide my hideous self. I was already developing a good story to tell when I was confronted by everyone else at school.

The truth is, there was no good explanation for this. I didn't even understand why they would do this to me. I would have rather had the belt again.

It didn't take long at school until my teacher approached me and took me out into the hall and wanted to know the meaning of this. I explained it to her and I know she was mortified.

She walked me to the principal's office. Mr. Walton came in. He wasn't smiling that big smile I saw the night of my speech when I mentioned his name. I could see his pain. At that moment, I actually felt I had his support; someone who just might save me from these people.

Mr. Walton asked me to sit just outside his office. I heard him on the phone and I couldn't hear much, but I did hear him raise his voice when he said, "But Dick, this is simply not right."

I wanted to hug Mr. Walton then and there. "Finally, someone is going to know what's going on at our house," I thought.

When Mr. Walton came out of his office, I saw that he was very upset. His voice was shaky. He told me I was to go back to class but if I needed to leave for any reason, I was allowed to come back to his office.

I felt so bad for him at that moment. But I had already been through the worst before school had even started. I could be resilient. I wouldn't let them break me. I went through the day and my strength was building. I felt I had won another battle because I survived whatever they wanted to throw at me.

I remember thinking, "What else are you gonna throw my way? You will not break me."

By this time, I was at an age where I was developing my own assumptions of what Dick and Gwen were doing to me; as their adopted child. I was convinced they wanted me dead. If not that, at least out of their lives. My brother Larry at the age of seven, was being reprimanded for something I don't remember. Dick literally told him to go upstairs and pack his bags and leave the house. He was serious too.

A lesson I self-taught myself was that no one, not even Dick or Gwen had ultimate power over me. I was convinced then and I remain convinced, to this day, that I had that power. I had to endure physical and emotional abuse because they were the parents and I was the child. But I would not become entirely powerless to them.

As a result, I developed a bit of an edge. I was careful not to showcase it to Dick, for fear of getting knocked around. I quietly learned to say to him and Gwen anytime they tried knocking me down, "Oh yeah, just watch me. I will do whatever you say I can't do."

In spite of them, I learned to achieve no matter how difficult the task was. In fact, I took extra precaution, strength or whatever it took to ensure I did not fail. I couldn't give them that power. It worked well for me then. It works well for me now, except my achievements are balanced with the proper motivation.

It wasn't long after the FILTH episode that I was put through another "test." That's how I saw all of this: tests. It made it easier for me to remain sane.

I had wanted to grow my hair a little longer. It was the seventies, right? I was trying to fit in and why not? I refused to let Gwen cut my hair. The next day Dick and Gwen teamed up and she handed Dick her hair pins and Dick made me put them in my hair to hold my bangs back; out of my face.

Again, this came with menacing instructions, "If you take these out I will kill you."

I think even my siblings were nervously laughing when they headed out to the school bus. I was embarrassed, but wouldn't show it. I can't remember what story I made up over why I was wearing "girls" hair pins but I don't remember it being as devastating as the "FILTH" debacle.

One late November day, us boys; Dan, Larry and I were outside. I guess having eight kids, we were pushed outside more often than not. It was a cold day and I remember the three of us were grumbling about having to be outside. In any event, Gwen came out and instructed us three boys to start raking the lawn. Out front of the farm was a big chestnut tree. I actually loved that tree. We always had to rake the lawn with heavy steel rakes. I bet they did a better job but I always found them to be heavy and just chewed up the lawn; making it harder to rake.

Despite being cold, we did as we were told, and only when we knew we were out of ear-shot did the three of us bitch and complain about how mean she was. We would never mouth back for fear of what would become of it.

Well, it wasn't long after we started to rake the lawn, a snow storm whipped up. It was blowing-in fast and furiously. We thought, great! We decided to stop for now, and started making our way to the shed to put the rakes away, when Gwen ran out.

"What do you think you're doing?"

Of course, it was obvious to us. It was snowing like rain and piling up on the lawn at a rapid pace.

She said sternly, "You will get back out there and finish the job."

We did. As we were raking, snow piling up on us like a blanket, we looked over towards the house and couldn't believe our eyes. In the big picture window we could see Gwen, Cheryl and Susan sitting in the window watching us, and drinking tea or hot chocolate.

Dan was furious, I remember.

I'm certain we all were, but this had become the norm for me. It was to be expected. Once I learned to expect the unexpected, I was fast becoming numb to it all. I put on my armour and chose to make the job a competition against the parents and win again and again. It wasn't Cheryl and Susan's fault at all of course. Back then, however, we blamed them all.

Despite being physically and emotionally abused repeatedly by Dick and Gwen over talking too much in class, I remained quite the talker, but learned how to use it in a positive way. I continued to enter the annual oratorical contests. I was getting better and by grade seven, I had found my stride. Gramma Barendregt continued to teach me tactics, and I loved the attention and love she gave me during all those hours I spent with her.

I often wondered if Gramma knew what was going on at our house. If she did, she kept quiet about it. So many times I wanted to tell her, but I didn't want to put her in an awkward position. After all, Dick was her eldest son and I had already learned that blood was thicker than water. Dick and Gwen made that abundantly clear by dividing our household into the Barendregt camp and the Pierson camp. We may have been adopted but we were not their kids and when we were perceived as having done something wrong we always heard "that's the Pierson inside of you." Either way, Gramma may have known more than I thought, but I'm not convinced it would have mattered. She shared her love unconditionally and I loved her dearly.

In grade seven, I finally won the top prize in the speech contest. I was so proud but alas, Dick and Gwen were not present. I was already used to that and so I enjoyed all the attention from everyone else in the room. After the trophies were handed out, an older man who happened to be one of the judges that evening came to me. He congratulated me and asked if I recognized him from church. Of course I did. He was the Minister of our church.

I was laughing under my breath because what I really wanted to say was, "No, sorry I don't, but I sure recognize your daughter."

His daughter was a really cute girl, and I think I paid more attention to her than his sermons.

He fueled my ego by telling me how I was such a strong orator. He then asked if I would consider reading the scriptures on the following Sunday.

I obliged. I did so because I knew I would make Gramma proud. She sat near the front pew every Sunday. I also knew I could possibly make an impression on Mary, the Minister's daughter.

Why wouldn't I do this?

I practiced the scripture reading he gave me nearly everyday. After all, I couldn't let him down. I had butterflies that Sunday and when called up to the pulpit, I rose and felt my legs were trembling and a bit of a cold sweat forming.

As I stepped up to the large pulpit, opened the bible and looked out to the congregation, I was calm.

I was perfectly relaxed.

I was in my element; seeking attention but in a positive way. At the end of the service that day, I can't count how many older women squeezed my cheeks and poured wonderful comments onto me. I was even snuck a smile from Mary, which really made it for me.

I was asked to come back and do it again. I accepted of course, and I became a weekly reader of the scriptures for the next year or so, I recall.

Upon reflection, I learned more about the bible because of my readings. In fact, I read the entire bible that year, from front to back. I found it interesting. I became fascinated with Christianity. I became reflective about life and my place in it, and why things happened the way they were happening to me.

Chapter 8

THE UNIVERSE FOUND ME IN THE RYE FIELD

That year I was thirteen years old. I don't know if it was because of my new-found attachment to heaven and God, but that summer it hit me: I remember going for a walk by myself. We had a pond at the far corner of the farm. To get there, I walked through the rye which at this time of year was as tall as my chest. I rustled the tips of the rye between my fingers and the rye would flow back and forth as I walked along; leaving a small trampled area where my feet had been.

I laid down in the field so nobody could see me and I looked up to the heavens.

I talked to God, then I talked to my mom. I was feeling sorry for myself. For at least the last two years of my life I had been building my resilience. I was building my thick skin armour to fend off anything Dick and Gwen could throw at me.

I was confident but something was happening as I lay there. I started feeling sorry for myself. I felt anger. I wanted things to be better for myself.

WHY WAS MY MOM NOT HERE? WHY DID SHE ABANDON ME?

I wept out loud. I didn't care because I figured no one would hear me. It was all my feelings that had been tucked away for the last few years pouring out of me. I am convinced now that it was the first time that I had actually come to terms with the loss of my mom. I had arrived at the sobering reality that she was never coming back; never going to hug me or kiss me; never going to comfort me. I don't remember how long I was crying and swearing and calling out, but I fell asleep. I woke up at least an hour later.

When I arose from the field, I made my way to the back of the farm to the pond. I felt better. I felt somehow closer to God and to Mom. I felt strong again. I was convinced I had just gone through a spiritual journey.

I have hung onto that afternoon all these years. I have come to know and understand a spiritual side of me that has made my life better and helped me to understand people so that I could help them too. Often, throughout our lives, we experience spiritual awakenings. I encourage you not to shove them away but rather to embrace them. Recognizing these signs is important for personal growth. I believe these awakenings are meant to teach us lessons that we need to explore in order to help ourselves and to help others.

I was able to identify this awakening as a lesson of hope and resilience. It was a coming of age; an understanding that I had to take ownership of my life and the direction in which I wanted to go. This isn't to suggest I was fully aware of my path, but perhaps a little more aware of my existence. I was reminded of my inner strength and knowledge, that I deserved better. The universe saw me that day and awoke in me a sense of my own self. I hope you will experience this several times in your lifetime. If you do, embrace it, explore it, and live happier.

As I have stated on more than one occasion, I feel blessed. I don't say this as if to suggest I'm more special than anyone else. I'm as equally flawed as the next. But, I have come to recognize a gift I have been given from the day I was born; a gift that truly allowed me to overcome the physical and emotional abuse I experienced as a young child, adolescent and adult.

The gift I possess is the gift of persistent joy and a genuine feeling of good cheer which stems from my faith in God and ripples through to my faith in people. This is a deep-rooted happiness that is inspired by understanding the trials I've faced as lessons learned. You might say that these were traumas, turned into experience by the gift of joy. These lessons, some painful and sad in nature, ultimately taught me the importance of imparting goodness, happiness and love to others.

The man I am today truly wants others to believe in themselves. I want you to know and to recognize that you have the strength and power to be the best person you can possibly be. As I age, this gift is more recognizable to me and my willingness to share it is more profound and far-reaching. I find my senses in this regard are more heightened now than ever before and I feel almost responsible to work with as many people as I possibly can to share this mindset.

We all have a gift. Are you aware of this? We're born with it. Some will argue our gifts are natural while others will say they're spiritual. I happen to believe they're both. I feel guided, at this moment, to share a verse from the bible, if I may.

---

1 Corinthians 12:7-11

But to each one is given the manifestation of the spirit. For the common good. For to one is given the word of wisdom through the spirit, and to another, the word of knowledge according to the same spirit; to another, faith by the same Spirit and to another gifts of healing by the one Spirit and to another, the effecting of miracles and to another, prophecy and to another the distinguishing of Spirits, to another various kinds of tongues and to another the interpretation of tongues. But one and the same Spirit works all these things, distributing to each one individually just as He wills.

That's quite an exhaustive "list" of spiritual gifts, isn't it? What if you don't find yourself in any of those? Does it mean you don't have a gift? Certainly not. Whether we call it a spiritual or a natural gift, I assure you, you have a gift or a talent.

Author Thomas Troward shares a very interesting dynamic about ourselves. One of his essays is entitled *Yourself*. I admit, when I was first introduced to this essay through the Working Writers Co. workshop, I was not hooked on it. But, after reading through Troward's words several more times, I was truly enlightened by it.

In his essay, Troward invites us to understand that we all have this "Essence-of-Life" from our very beginning. We're born with it. He further invites us to learn to be happy with ourselves and it takes less strain and strife than trying to be somebody else. We need to be content with our "God-given" talent. Most importantly, he teaches us not to force it. It will naturally spring up within us. All we have to do is recognize it within ourselves and allow it to manifest into our own inner peace and power. I encourage you to find this essay. Read it, re-read it and I am certain you will be transformed by it. I have been transformed by it and my universe has opened-up broader than even I could have expected, ever since.

I am happier, more patient with myself, and towards others. Troward's essay is indeed a "promise" of inner power that is inexhaustible. We can't use up this power. In fact, the more good we do for ourselves and others, the more good that comes back. I have come to understand that "Giving is Getting." It's not a selfish understanding at all. It's a pay-it-forward reality. We receive more love, happiness and comfort by giving than we can ever imagine. I hope you try this little experiment and find the same inspiration as I have.

Chapter 9

GO FORWARD, EVEN IF YOU DON'T KNOW WHY

By the end of high school, which was the summer of 1981, I was finding it increasingly difficult at home with the Barendregts. Nonetheless, it was decided that I would attend college. My older adopted brother, Mike, had attended Ridgetown Agricultural College in 1978 and graduated in 1980. Ridgetown was known for its agricultural production management. Dick felt that I would be better suited for business and was consequently enrolled into Centralia Agricultural College with a major in business management.

That summer, before I began the fall semester at college, Dick and Gwen Barendregt must have known it was time for me to move out of the house. I credit them for allowing me the opportunity to live in a home located on a property they owned; one that operated as a farm supply business in town. I think that, for Dick, having me live on the premises of his business was a cheap form of security for his business and equipment sitting in the yard. Either way, it worked out for me too.

Ken and I quickly made the premises into a bachelor style pad, complete with a wagon wheel coffee table and walls that were overlaid with barn boards, salvaged from somewhere. It was heaven for both of us. We had each saved enough money from summer jobs to own our own cars which gave us both independence. I had a girlfriend, whom I had over quite frequently. Ken was very accommodating but I sensed a few times that I was pushing the boundaries of his own space in the house.

In the meantime, I went off to college but was back at our pad on most weekends. Ken was just bumping around trying to find his own path. It always felt good, coming back to our safe haven, to catch-up. Ken would fish a lot and I think we had a month straight of eating his fresh caught pickerel, fried potatoes, and corn. These meals were reminiscent of our camping days.

On family occasions, celebrations, or holiday dinners, I would show up at the Pfeffer home just like one of the kids. It was here that I felt most myself. Regardless of whether I was Stephen Pierson, or Steven Barendregt, at the Pfeffer's, I was my best self.

By the summer, following my first year of college, I learned that I had not achieved enough credits to continue-on with the graduate program. At around the same time, I learned that Dick expected I would work as a hand on the farm, after I graduated from college. I wanted better than that. I deserved better than that. I was confused and, frankly, quite disappointed. *Why was I attending business college just to be a farm hand?* I thought.

With this expectation on me, I didn't have any interest in going back to college and decided to consider my options. Ken and I were still hanging out in the bachelor pad so at least I had a place to hang my hat. It was like old times in many ways, but I think we both knew things needed to change and we needed to get on with our lives. We spoke about it on several occasions.

Ken knew he had to decide what he was going to do with his life. I recognized the same but I needed time to think about my future; a future that clearly wasn't going where I hoped it might. A lot of our conversations around this topic were fun. Ken was a very bright student. I was always amazed at how intelligent he was in high school math and sciences. We were complete opposites in this way. He struggled with English, writing and social studies where I found them easy and interesting. I struggled with maths and sciences. The truth is, neither of us wanted to do what our parents did. Ken's dad had worked his way into the corporate offices but started on the plant floor of a large international manufacturing company. I didn't want to be a farm hand.

Ken's brother Johnny was an electrician and Ken figured he could see himself doing that. At least he had a vague idea, whereas I did not.

After many conversations and dreaming, we did the only "natural" thing that allowed us to put off "becoming an adult" a while longer. In the fall of 1982, I was ostensibly on my own. I had my own pad, my own car and my own bank account. At least I thought I had my own bank account.

Ken and I took our money from summer work and went off on a Can-Rail pass from Ontario through the Prairies, the Rockies, and into beautiful British Columbia. We were exercising our independence. Our plan was to work in the oil sands and make lots of money. While we never spent one day working anywhere, much less the oil sands, it was a wonderful coming-of-age trip for me. I had never seen Canada the way one can see through a rail pass. The great thing about the rail pass, is that it allowed us to hop on and off wherever we decided to stay over and hang out for a while.

I couldn't believe how many small towns were scattered across Ontario as we headed west. Initially, it was quaint and interesting but after the fiftieth stop, one small town bled into the next and the journey seemed to go on and on. By the time we hit the Prairies and the never-ending canola fields, I was growing weary of the ride. I did enjoy seeing the colourful grain elevators that broke up the vast endless fields of the Prairies.

My independence was broken by a visit to the local bank to withdraw some of my money. The long arm of Dick had reached me all the way out West. The bank teller looked at me and said I had to speak to the manager. That was odd, I thought. I didn't know anyone out here and certainly was sure that no one knew me. The manager advised me that he received a call from the bank manager in my hometown. Right then,

I knew it. Dick was controlling me once again. He got into my bank account and decided I was spending too much of MY money. I was hopping mad. How could the bank even allow him into my business? So much for MY bank account and MY money. It bothered me that he had to get his nose into my business. It reminded me of his reach and his influence. From that day forward, I felt Dick was there looking over my shoulder. It tainted the trip.

My mind wandered endlessly as I looked out the train window. I would play many scenes in my mind about my future. I listened to the best of Simon & Garfunkel on my walkman. Those songs pierced my soul; opened my mind. I reminisced about my earlier life; how long it seemed since Mom was gone. I realised I was unable to really picture her face anymore. That bothered me. The grey skies and the rain pounding against the train window only made me more depressed. Here I was, eighteen years old. I felt enormous pressure to be someone; to do something. If I was that person again today, I would tell him to slow down; stop feeling sorry for himself. There's lots of time to get it right. Take that time to weigh all your options and it will come to you.

But I wasn't that person then. I knew being sad was ok. Feeling sorry for myself, was not. I had been heartbroken over the loss of my mom. I didn't know how heartbroken I was when she died. How could I? I was only seven.

I remember finding my way up to the sky car on the train. This was the train car that had its entire roof made of glass. Even with the grey skies and pounding rain, the sky car made me feel closer to God. I always drifted towards God (and perhaps my deceased mom) when I was sad. Allowing myself to feel sad was a way for me to self heal too, I thought. I was so fortunate to have this insight as a young adult. I truly never knew where it came from. Secretly, I always felt it was a gift from God for the misfortune of losing my mom so early in life.

After about an hour in the sky car, my self pity; reduced to sadness, made way for optimism. I started evaluating some of my key strengths. How could I leverage those into a better life plan for myself? I knew I was **resilient.** Having been through all that I had at such an early age and still **passionate** about life, proved that. I had learned through my short life to **communicate** effectively with my peers as well as my elders. I knew I had a great sense of **humour.** I was often coined the class clown. I was initially bothered by the comment from my mother's letter that stated "Steven, you are my funny clown, but sometimes you have to remember not everything is funny." From an early age, I took it as a signal to be more serious in my life.

Thank goodness I eventually recognized it as a motivator to bring happiness to others. Lastly, I knew I was a **leader.** I knew this from my experience in high school and the encouragement I received from others to be a leader in sports and as student council president.

Just as God had planned it, and without me even noticing as I was deep in my self evaluation, the sky broke and opened up to allow the sun to pierce through the fractured clouds into the sky car. The warmth pressed onto me and sent a shudder of tingles throughout my whole body. I felt closer to God in that moment than I believe I have ever felt in my life; even to this day. It was a special moment. I was blessed and I knew it.

I looked out the train car window and saw a deep gorge as we seemed to be ascending into the heavens on rails. I knew we must be getting closer to the Rockies. Ken and I had already agreed that when we got to the mountains, we had to be in the sky car to really take them in. I thought I should go get him as I knew we were approaching them soon. A few moments later Ken showed up with a big grin on his face. "Well, what have you been doing up here?" It was as if he knew I needed some alone time. I answered with a grin, "finding myself, I guess." All of a sudden it seemed as though the rest of the passengers hopped into the sky car to take-in the Rockies. What a sight they were. I had just been through a personal journey with God and he followed it up with the Rockies! I was absolutely breathless as I marvelled at the sheer beauty and magnificence of them. I am reminded of a phrase I had read before:

Never blame anyone in your life.

Good people give you happiness. Bad people give you experience. The worst people give you a lesson. And the best people give you memories.

I think this message held very true to what I had experienced in my life up to this point. I would spend the rest of my years perfecting the philosophy.

By 1983, both Ken and I had made plans. Ken would start college at Sir Sandford Fleming in Lindsay, Ontario, and I decided to start all over at Centralia College. This time, I was doing it with my own vision and my own reason for being there; a decision that would shape my life, forever.

Ken and I stayed in touch, mostly through his family gatherings from time to time. But without question, this would be the longest gap of being apart that we had ever incurred. It was good for both of us. I had never been apart from the Pfeffer family since the day I met Ken. As the years ebbed and flowed, we didn't see each other that often, but we stayed in touch.

I have been fortunate to have Ken stand up as my best man. Ken has always been my protector. As we got older, Ken became much stronger than I, but we still had fun rough housing. He could toss me around like a rag doll. Like his mother, however, he had and still has a wonderfully genuine laugh that makes you laugh when you hear it. He has a heart of gold. I knew from the day I met Ken, he had my back; I could ask him for anything, anytime and he would oblige. The movie *Braveheart* reminds me of our relationship. Do you remember the William Wallace (played by Mel Gibson) character who had a childhood friend? He was the big burly redhead with a flowing red beard. Strong as an ox and a big laugh. His eyes were true and kind. That is Ken, and he's still that person. Who else would be my best man, but Ken? As we stood together at the altar that day, I knew I had a lifetime friend and we were both right where we were meant to be.

I have been blessed to watch my Pfeffer siblings have children of their own and become known to those children as Uncle Steve. It brings me a tremendous amount of pride.

All the while, I've spoken very little of Ken's dad, Jack. This in no way reflects a lack of love and respect for him. He was a quiet man; a principled person. I secretly and quietly called him "Dad." I learned more from Dad Pfeffer in my adult years than I ever gave him credit for.

I learned from him that being quiet doesn't mean you're disinterested. It doesn't mean that you don't love. Listening enables one to thoroughly hear the whole story; and only then, make a decision. Lessons I learned from Dad Pfeffer weren't taught by talking but by me just watching and learning and applying this to my everyday life. I have often rushed into things without too much thought. His lessons taught me to slow down and consider everything and make informed decisions.

These lessons mean more to me now than I realized back then. I find myself using many of these lessons today as a coach and mentor to young professionals.

I especially instill the need to listen carefully. "Just be observational. Allow your clients to share their story. Don't interject too soon. When we listen, we allow ourselves to be more attentive, more empathetic and more helpful when it's our time to impart advice."

I spent countless moments watching Dad Pfeffer create beautiful things from wood. He was very talented that way. Ken and his dad didn't always see things the same way but they were actually more alike than either of them knew, in my opinion. Ken learned the art and skill of a wood craftsman; just like his dad.

I know that Dad Pfeffer loved all of his children. What was amazing for me was a knowingness that he loved me too. The year Ken and I left to travel West on our Can-rail passes, I wrote him a personal note. The note expressed to him that I loved him. I thanked him for allowing me to be a part of his family. He kept that note until the day he died. Mother gave me the note after he died.

Only a few months earlier, we had attended the funeral of Ken's brother John. It was a hot summer day so Dad stayed inside the truck with the air conditioner on so his breathing wasn't impaired. I was in the seats with the rest of the family but I was watching him. He gazed from the truck window at his entire family. It seemed to me that as his gaze stretched out over the seated family members, he was taking inventory of his own life. It was as if I was reading his mind as I watched him. His eyes reflected the love, the laughter, the pain and the regrets. I was watching him and hoping what he felt was pride and love. He deserved to feel that way in my opinion.

Since his death on July 16, 2021, I have come to realize, all over again, just how important the Pfeffer family was and is to me. While Ken and I remain close friends, I have rekindled friendships with the rest of the siblings too. I speak to Mother every week and, for the first time in a long time, I spent Christmas 2021 back at the Pfeffer homestead with mother and siblings, nieces and nephews, and the whole gang. It was as if I had never left. I felt safe and happy again. I was reminded how fragile life really is. Sitting there with everyone, I felt it important that my children, Lindsay and Matthew, also reconnect. I reflected on so many wonderful memories Matthew and Lindsay had growing up with the Pfeffer clan when they were younger. When they were younger, Ken's parents were known to me as Mother and Father and to my children as Gramma and Grandpa Pfeffer. Gramma Pfeffer still to this day never forgets to send them a birthday card. Both Lindsay and Matt have become busy in their own lives and drifted apart. Each of them still speak fondly of the Pfeffer family which I appreciate.

Most of all, I knew I was in the right place and I felt loved. I learned how to love better in my own life as a result of being a part of this family.

Chapter 10

A PRODUCT OF OUR ENVIRONMENT?

I often felt desperate to understand why we were being moved around so much. It was this constant moving, this constant unpredictability of my future that made me feel powerless. These days, one might say I'm a bit of a planner. I organize my own stuff. Even managing my own company for twenty years, I always had a hand in what I was doing. I remember that feeling of not having much choice. I suppose that's why I exercise my choices today. What a luxury so many of us take for granted.

My younger experience of moving between the two orphanages perhaps set the stage for my need for control; which, at times, was beneficial and sometimes equally as detrimental. The unsettling experience shaped me into a bit of a controlling person. But I wanted to, at least, control my own disciplines. I learned early in life to align with positive people, circumstances, and environments. I learned to avoid negativity, to drift more towards positivity, while avoiding negative people, circumstances and environments. It was a coping mechanism; a means to keep things in order and in control. I would learn later in life to seek out positive influences and influencers. Many people whom I will talk about in this book made that positive difference and contributed to my success in life. Somehow, some way, I found or perhaps attracted a score of positive people, all of whom had a profoundly positive influence on my life. What a well balanced person I've become in spite of all I've gone through and all that I went through, right?

Wrong!

Earlier in my life, sometime in my early twenties when I was starting out in my career as a commercial banker, I was relentless in my pursuit of success. I had my eye on the prize, everyday. I was laser-focused at the expense of others around me who I thought may get in my way. I accepted almost any challenge put in front of me and I poured everything into being successful.

My new bosses became my "Dick and Gwen" in the sense that these were people I would attempt to prove wrong if they merely hinted at the suggestion that there was something I couldn't accomplish. I would now prove them wrong if they even remotely thought I couldn't do the task given to me. I was competing with talented young men and women who had better pedigrees, on paper, than I did. Nearly everyone I was working with had, at the very least, an undergraduate business degree and many had the infamous "MBA," Masters of Business Administration. I had a college diploma in business administration. That's all I could afford and even then I had to borrow money to finish college. I was competing with these "smart" and talented individuals, but I had other tools: I used my qualitative talents to succeed. In my first few years with the Bank of Montreal, I made a name for myself and was rewarded with the President's Award of Excellence. This got me recognized by the Executive of the bank. I was invited to the executive dining room to have lunch with the CEO of the bank and other executives. From that point on, I was hooked. I wanted that better life for myself and I would drive myself deeper and deeper into my work; sometimes at the expense of my family.

As a husband and father, I was more controlling and wanted to "fix" things if they were 'broken." I was a problem-solver more than a listener. My children would call me out on this more often as their problems became more complex with their age. It wasn't easy for me to change. I just wanted to fix their problems and move on. Sometimes, people just need to be heard. It took me many years to learn this. I'm grateful to those close to me who were patient with me and helped me learn this. I feel I have become better at this today than ever before.

A Product Of Our Environment?

When I was about thirty years old, I was invited to compete with other talented young professionals in a group study exchange through International Rotary. I was living in London, Ontario, at the time and really only had a brief understanding of what the Rotary Club was all about. In any event, I was a young "up-and-comer" in the business community and my profile caught the attention of some Rotarians. This would be an international exchange to Germany; a vocational ambassadorship between our countries. Three young people from Canada and two from the United States of America would be selected to represent the team. Since doing well thus far in my career, I was more confident now that I was worthy to be selected as one of the participants. What an honour it was to go. As a young husband and new father, it was even more surprising that my wife supported the six week exchange.

I was representing my vocation as a banker and as a result I was billeted to new Rotarian families each week. In my case, I stayed with some of the most powerful men in the German banking industry. These were CEOs of massive banks, and what an opportunity it was. Again, I was introduced to luxury beyond anything I had ever experienced. I was discussing world politics, business, and human interest topics with these powerful men and their families. It was around the time the "wall" separating Eastern and Western Germany had fallen. We were allowed to go into Eastern Germany. This was very real for me. Eastern Germany was still back in the fifties. Buildings were run down and, everything seemed dirty. I saw people who, for the first time, had been given their freedom. This would be the the first time they had access to money or at least the ability to earn their own money. Free enterprise at its finest was right before me.

I was asked by several people when I returned from this exchange, "What did you learn over in Germany?" I learned how ashamed these people were of their past with respect to anything related to Hitler. I learned that it was wrong to keep families away from each other for so many years by constructing a wall to keep them apart. But mostly, what I learned on this exchange was about myself. I learned that what I thought was a difficult childhood: living in the orphanage, having to find food to eat, crying for the affection of a mother who was no longer there for me, was a realization that so many others had or have it just as bad or even worse than me. I realized that all of the challenges somehow made me who I am today. Having to survive only made me stronger. While I knew I still carried "baggage" as a result, I would overcome any obstacle in my way with pride.

As a leader today, managing a group of talented young professionals, I am grateful to be viewed by them as an effective coach and mentor. Over the years, I have honed my people skills into effective motivational coaching skills. It comes naturally to me because I am genuinely invested in the wellbeing of the people I lead. I am accountable to their success. I communicate this early and often which has proven highly successful for all parties.

One of the initiatives I started within our office was to implement a Reward & Recognition program. Each month, two individuals are nominated by their own peers to receive this award. It was important that I, as leader, empowered them. I have learned that empowerment builds leadership and accountability, and this program works. The criteria was purposefully left open with an emphasis on living our values in a way that positively impacts both our peers and our customers. Emphasis is placed on living the values we all want to live by that impacts our peers as much as our customers.

One of my mentors always says, "leadership is a tough business." No doubt, it is, at times, but the rewards of strong and effective leadership are powerfully motivating to keep working hard at being a good leader.

I would like to share some unsolicited remarks I have received from some of the talented professionals I work with.

From Sandra: *"The last month I have had a number of situations where I needed some guidance. The advice you provided was truly invaluable. Your leadership goes above any other leader I have had in my career. You care about each member of our team and always make time to check in and see how everyone is doing; not just within their role, but personally. I truly feel that this motivates each of us to push ourselves and succeed in everything we do. Thank you so much for everything you do, not just for me but our whole team".*

From Peggy: *"As you may or may not know, I am too shy to speak out in front of people (I get tongue tied)!, but I want to let you know that I think you are an AMAZING leader. You listen, you support, you empathize, you communicate, you're forward and to the point (instead of beating around the bush). You CARE and I love your sense of humour. I can't think of anyone else who I would rather have to lead our Business Banking Centre than you.*

From Simon: *"I've had a lot of personal reflection over the last couple of weeks leading up to this (milestone) birthday. I just thought I would pass along that you are one of the people I appreciate."*

These are wonderful reminders of how I know I'm on the right path as a leader. I continue to train myself to be a more effective listener. I talk routinely about leadership with my team. I believe that empowerment of others drives accountability. This is how, I believe we build effective leaders together.

As a minor league soccer coach, I practiced my ability to be an effective leader with the players on my team. During the "draft," I announced to the other coaches I would prove that I could win the championship without any of the "star" players. The other coaches laughed and joked, but I was sincere in my statement. I immediately built trust with my players by sending emails to them every week before the game. I invited them to reflect on their commitment to themselves, their family, and then to their team. Within 4 weeks, I could see a change in the players. During the first five minutes, pre-game, I always formed a huddle. Not to discuss our game but to ask everyone how their week was. The team was accountable to each other but at the same time, they were committed to their personal achievements. Suffice it to say, we won the championship that year. We had the "all-star" team in heart, passion and commitment to one another. No one wanted to let the other down.

I continue to communicate with my work team, early and often, as a tool for coaching. In a highly competitive environment, I have developed skills to motivate people that empower them to succeed and ingrain in them that "their team's success is their own success".

Chapter 11

TOBACCO: I AIN'T A QUITTER

Growing up on a large tobacco farm meant there were always chores to do. Summer meant tobacco harvest and harvest meant a good-paying summer job. I was twelve years old and wanted to get in on making the $75 dollars per day "picking" tobacco. It wasn't an easy job but I thought I was ready and quite able to do it.

I asked Dick if I could pick tobacco and he told me, "Not likely until the following year."

I was upset and decided I would find my own job. I biked a short distance up the road to Uncle Howard Cross' farm. Howard and Agnes Cross owned and operated a tobacco farm too. Agnes was actually Dick's aunt on his mother's side.

I thought, "This will be easy to get a job; after all, he's family."

I remember Howard; he always carried a soft smile and had what I remember to be a warm personality. I rode up his lane and saw him out around the barn.

I hopped off my bike and tried to look as big and as confident as I possibly could.

I boldly claimed: "I think I would be really good at picking tobacco."

Howard smiled, as I knew he would. Then, he asked the question I knew would kill any chance of winning the job.

"Ok, what does your dad say to that? Is he willing to hire you?"

I sheepishly confirmed that Dick had suggested I wait a year. That was it. My hopes were dashed, but my spirit was still defiant.

I was riding my bike back to the farm, and as I drew closer to home, I grew more upset. I decided to ride past the farm, cycle two more concessions, which took me to another farm that was managed by a man named Ken Kish. Ken was a sharecropper. A sharecropper is a tenant farmer who rents the farm and a share of the crop is paid to the farm owner.

Again, I approached Mr. Kish with the same bravado and an aim to impress him with my abilities. I stated that I'd be a real benefit to his operations. I decided to tell him the truth, that my dad was unwilling to hire me but I thought he was wrong.

Mr. Kish had a wide open smile but he didn't laugh out loud.

He replied, "Well, I'm not sure if the work will be too hard for you, Steve. But I'll tell you what: I have a couple young pickers who drop a lot of leaves when they're picking tobacco. Do you think you could try walking behind these guys and pick-up the dropped leaves?"

I think my grin was even wider than Mr. Kish's grin from earlier-on. He even agreed to pay me $30 dollars per day. That was about half what the pickers were making, but a good start for me.

Wow! I'd done it. I was never prouder than at that moment. I parked my bike right then and there and started that afternoon. At the end of the day, I was beat. It was a lot of walking up and down the field, bending over, picking up leaves, one round after another. But I didn't care. I was pumped with adrenaline at the prospect of telling Dick what I had accomplished that afternoon. I couldn't wait until dinner time. I said nothing to anyone and just waited for the moment Dick asked the question he often asked at the dinner table.

"Well, what did you do today?"

Tobacco: I Ain't A Quitter

I think I nearly lept out of my chair when I blurted out "I GOT MYSELF A JOB TODAY."

I think Dick learned something about me that day. I think he learned that I wasn't a quitter. I think he learned that I had good negotiation skills, beyond my years. I had hoped he'd be proud of me for being resourceful. I sensed that he was and it made me feel like I could achieve anything.

Near the end of that summer, one of Mr. Kish's pickers had to leave to go back to school and couldn't stay to finish the harvest. I was given the nod, and you'd better believe I wasn't going to mess it up. I finished the last six or seven weeks at $75 dollars per day. That was when I truly learned the power of saving money.

By thirteen years old, I was working in the tobacco harvest. I could have had a job anywhere with anybody by that point. I even got a job at Uncle Howard's the next year. At the end of the week we would receive a brown envelope with a cash payment for the week. Six days of work meant $450.

Suddenly, I had more money than I had ever seen before.

I bought my own record player, cassette deck, and stereo speakers for my room. I had enough money to buy my own clothes. Getting ready for high school was exciting. Buying the latest and greatest in clothes was not an issue for me.

I remember having all my newly purchased clothes and shoes all set up for high school. Then something unbelievable happened. The evening before the first day of school I couldn't find my new clothes or shoes anywhere.

Where did they go?

Dan's were also missing. Something was wrong and we looked everywhere, but they were nowhere to be found. Grudgingly, we had to wear our old things. Dan and I commiserated, and figured we knew what had happened. Gwen had taken our clothes and shoes and she hid them from us. *And yet, how could we prove this without getting knocked around for even suggesting such a thing?*

We Pierson kids had been advised by Gwen that we were not allowed in the parents' bedroom. Her own kids were allowed, but not us. Not being allowed in, Dan and I had to find a way to prove our new clothes were in her closet. We waited for a time when no one was in the house to investigate for ourselves.

The stakes were high, but Dan and I knew what we would find.

I dashed into her room, while Dan kept the lookout.

I opened Dick and Gwen's closet door, dug around; and at the back of her closet, I felt something familiar: our new clothes. We found them, and now we had proof. This presented a new dilemma, however. How would we get them back without causing more harm to ourselves by entering the forbidden zone?

In the end, we decided to take our new purchases out, and return them to our rooms.

The next day before school, we came down the stairs, wearing our new clothes.

I felt so scared on the one hand, but so validated on the other hand, when I saw Gwen's face. I announced before she even said anything, "Oh, we found our lost clothes and shoes; thank goodness."

I'm certain that pissed her off, but what else could she do? Any objection would have been an admission of guilt as to why she hid our stuff in the first place.

I learned a lesson through the experience though: two wrongs don't make a right very often; but in our case, her *wrong* by hiding our stuff and our *wrong* by going into the forbidden bedroom worked out just fine! I was building my inner confidence and gaining an ability to problem solve, not to mention an understanding of psychology.

"Take the good with the bad," is something I used to repeat quite often. And that's because I've found that life has a certain balance.

Chapter 12

A Little Help from My Friends

I was grateful that during my years at the Barendregt's, I had good influences to teach me things and to encourage me sufficiently enough to push me through the tough and often unexplainable times. My primary outside early influences were the Pfeffer family, whom I've spent time describing. But there were others.

Another couple was John and Diane Verbruggen. I used to babysit their boys; Mike, Bob, Kevin, and Scott. All are grown-up with their own families now but I remain in contact with Bob, more so than the others.

John and Diane moved down our way sometime when I was a teenager. They were both hard working. John started with one truck and a contract. Eventually, he added another truck and his hard work paid off. Today they own and operate a highly successful transportation company. John preferred farming more than trucking and so he bought several acres of farmland in the region and ended-up owning some significant land.

These two people were wonderful sounding boards for me. Their hard work ethos rubbed off on me. I saw what they were able to achieve and they motivated me.

I remember the time I was going to get my driver's license. Like any new driver at the age of 16, this was a pretty exciting time. I had been (illegally) driving the farm trucks and tractors from farm to farm for a few years, so I felt pretty confident.

Gwen had gone out of her way to announce "The likelihood of you getting your license on the first try is slim to none."

Diane Verbruggen, by contrast, encouraged me so heartily that I felt confident and wanted to prove Gwen wrong and Diane right. I passed on my first attempt.

One of the first cars I ever bought required a co-signer for the bank loan. John and Diane Verbruggen offered me their signature and I was able to buy the car. I knew it wasn't a big strain on their finances, but that wasn't the point. Through their faith in me, I learned that having trust and integrity were worth far more than any amount of money.

I decided then to never let them down, and I didn't. When I was in college, I was working three jobs to pay for what I had; mostly living in residence as my "home" and in my car when I wasn't able to use the residence. One day, I received a letter from the college administration that I owed money for the ensuing semester and needed to pay immediately to avoid being kicked out.

What was I going to do? I know I could have asked Mr. Pfeffer and he would have given me the funds, but I didn't want to ask. I tried every possible way but was coming up short. I turned to John and Diane Verbruggen again. I explained what I needed.

Without even another breath, John looked at Diane and said, "Mother, you better write this boy a cheque right away."

We agreed that I would pay the amount back, in full, when I received my first paycheck by being gainfully employed the following spring.

Have you ever had someone believe in you so unconditionally? Or more importantly, have you ever shown this level of support to someone else? I can tell you first hand that the Verbruggen's belief in me likely changed the trajectory of my life. Today, I look for every opportunity to support young people. Are you looking for such opportunities? I ask you to consider what kind of legacy you would like to leave. I assure you there are young Steven Barendregts everywhere who are trying, hoping, praying, hustling, and wishing that things would just work out. They're not looking for a handout, just as I wasn't, but would gratefully accept a hand up.

I graduated that spring of 1985 and started my first job at the bank as a Commercial Account Manager. Proudly, I went to pay John and Diane back for what they had loaned me. I remember handing them a cheque for the full amount.

To my surprise, another moment of grace was granted to me.

John looked at Diane and then back to me and said, "Why don't you just keep that money to help you get started?"

I could have cried. I may have; I don't remember.

I looked back to John.

I said, "We had a deal and I intend to keep it. So please take this money with my utmost love and respect."

He did, and I know that gained me the respect I wanted to earn from them. We remain dear friends to this day. I regret we don't see each other as often, but I think of them often and I'm grateful to share our story. They taught me that struggle is only temporary, and that hard work, integrity, and passion will overcome many obstacles. They believed in me and that counted.

I have been so fortunate to have people weave their way in and out of my life. I often reflect on those years with the sense of how the universe provided. I was so down and out at times in my life, but there were always *angels* who showed up when I needed them.

Another family I was blessed to spend time with was Bill and Valerie Cron. Bill was an honest, hard-working farmer down near where I lived and grew up. We shared the same birthday which was a neat revelation I felt. Bill was quieter but he had a calming confidence about him and it resonated with me. I enjoyed being around a father-like figure and not having to feel like I needed to walk on eggshells again. Bill and Valerie had two children; Nicole and Kevin. They were little tikes running around the farm and they too made me feel welcome into their home. I know I could have stayed as long as I needed and looking back, I wish I had taken more time to hang with Bill. He was an awesome male figure for me and would be for anyone who had the pleasure of knowing him no doubt. I found myself once again, appreciating how wonderful it would have been to have Bill as a dad growing up.

Valerie was a fireball; still is. I wasn't sure exactly what Valerie did back when we met, but she was more of a lobbyist, and had a way of managing people better than anyone I had ever met before. She was a real go-getter and I loved being around her. I will never forget that every time that phone rang, Valerie would grab a smoke and get it going before answering the call. Years later Valerie quit smoking but I don't know how she ever overcame that vice; she lit up, and then she ignited conversation with her natural blazing passion.

I was attending college when I was introduced to the Cron's through my girlfriend at the time. She had a long-term relationship with Bill and Valerie and while I was never too sure, I think the Cron's really helped my girlfriend in her time of need. I was living half the time in my college residence and when college was out for the summer months, I would live half the time in my car or loafing on someone else's couch.

My girlfriend explained my situation to Bill and Valerie and they opened their home to me. It was awkward at first because I felt I should be looking after myself. They made me feel so welcome. I can't recall when I had finally moved out, but the Cron's were another example for me of how a family could work together and support one another.

These were such fundamental lessons, but important to me then and even more so now. Prior to 2020, it had been many years since I've seen Bill and Valerie. Thanks to social media, we reconnected. I gleefully invited them to my cottage on the lake since they were to be in the area with their camper September 19, 2020.

Imagine, it was a full forty years later when I hugged them both. It was far too long for me to wait to tell them in a heartfelt way: "THANK YOU." I was choked-up telling them as they sat at the harvest table that sits in the family room of our cottage. I felt grateful for having been given this opportunity to share with them just how impactful they were to me at that stage in my life. Never wait to tell someone how appreciated they are or how much they mean to you. Certainly don't wait as long as I did in this case.

As a leader today, I often suggest to my team the importance of saying 'thank you". Those words should be said to anyone; regardless of one's rank or fortune. It shows compassion, understanding and most importantly, respect.

Saying thank you to others who have made a difference in your life stems from the principle ***"By giving more, we receive more."***

My being able to say thank you to Bill and Valerie Cron, even as late as it was, provided me with a sense of genuine comfort. When we say thank you to someone, we are contributing to their self esteem. It tells them how much you appreciate them. Your appreciation confirms their place in your heart and it validates your genuine feelings.

Saying thank you, even for those who have a difficult time showing or expressing emotion, invites you to validate your own self esteem and builds confidence. You should try it yourself. I've had many benefactors along the way; people who gave unselfishly. I'm so genuinely thankful for all they've done, and have done my best to thank each and every one of them. None of them were looking for a thing in return from me. I have learned to adopt that same unselfish thinking. Funny enough, I've often felt that my giving to others is almost a selfish act because I feel so darn good in doing so.

Do you remember the scene in the Charles Dickens novel, *A Christmas Carol*? It's the scene when Scrooge wakes from his dreams and is so giddy with happiness by repenting his ways and giving back to those he had wronged. He felt guilty about being so giddy and happy. If we simply make giving and thanking a regular part of our daily life, it no longer feels awkward. Our light persona shines through in everything we do. Try it, you will be happier in no time. Your leadership quotient will rise and, like Scrooge, you will be loved more.

Over the next few pages, you'll find images from my childhood that provide you with a glimpse into what it was like growing up...

My Mother and Father on their wedding day

A Little Help From My Friends

My siblings and I. Approx. 1968.
Back row: Gord, (Sue) Sandi, Bill.
Middle row: Me on the left and Dan on my right.
Youngest brother Larry in front

Steve Age 10 (1973)

Steve age 11, 1974

Steve at age 12 circa 1975

A Little Help From My Friends

You will recall my writing about our campsites. Notice the walkways from tent to tent made of wooden branch sticks

We would often bring other high school chums camping. Here circa 1978-9 is Ken with the fry pan and Paul

Camping 1978 washing dishes

Brother Larry and I with my cool music headphones at March 1979 camp

Annual Camping trip March circa 1978 homemade table

A Little Help From My Friends

College graduation 1985 awarded Ministry of Agriculture and Food Leadership Award

My summer job for the Ministry of Agriculture & Food press release as the new Agricrew boss for Middlesex and Lambton counties, 1984

Brother Larry and his infamous chicken coup

Dan and I

My son Matthew with Grampa (Jack) Pfeffer. Christmas 1999.
Jack Pfeffer also celebrated his birthday Christmas day

My son Matthew and Gramma (Joyce) Pfeffer Christmas 1999

Me and Gramma Barendregt circa 1997

1999 Gramma Barendregt, Lindsay and Matt. Lindsay had just finished delivering her school speech for Gramma and I

Sandra and my engagement picture 2010.
Located at her grandfather's original home in Italy

A Little Help From My Friends

A year following our engagement, we were married Oct 1, 2011

Sandra and I at the Lake

Hope Stock Farm with the Kent family. I believe circa 1983-4.
I learned a lot from Punch Kent here

Hope Stock Farm 1984. Lise Kent and myself

February 2016 Punch Kent with Mare, Elusive Hope

John and Diane Verbruggen 50th wedding anniversary Nov 2022

Bill, Valerie Cron with me at the cottage Summer 2021

Ken and Steve 2022

Pfeffer family Xmas 2021. L to R back row: Ken, Mother, Joy, Darlene. Front row Diane and me

Danielle and Amanda and I at the Lake Summer 2022

Lindsay and I Fall 2021

Matt and I Fall 2022

Us Pierson siblings June 2022 from left to right, Larry, me, Dan, Sandi, Bill, and Gord

Chapter 13

FROM EGGSHELLS TO ICE CREAM

Despite walking on eggshells so often living with the Barendregt's, there were also good times. When I was thirteen, Dick came home with a school bus. He informed us that we would all need to sand the bus down to be repainted and converted into a camper. It was so much fun as all of us kids grabbed our pieces of sandpaper and sanded away the day. We were all covered in school bus yellow, but we didn't care. It was a project that allowed us all to contribute and I'm sure I learned some team building skills that day. I don't even recall an argument with anyone.

We were all focused on the prize when the bus was finished: a trip to Disneyworld in Florida. In the end, the bus was painted red and white. With all eight of us kids piled into the bus, we pretended we were the famous sitcom family in those days: *The Partridge Family*.

Gwen and their youngest child, Susan, flew ahead of us by airplane. The rest of us piled in the bus while Dick drove. The eight track tapes were playing great seventies songs from Johnny Cash, to Merle Haggard and Elvis Presley. I remember it being loads of fun. I do have to give Dick credit: I can't imagine being the sole driver all that way with seven kids riding and singing along.

Disneyworld was a blast and my most memorable moment was with my sister Sandi. We had not gotten along well for the last few years. I expect it was due more to an age gap between us, and the male versus female thing. But on that trip, we bonded again; and as best as I can remember, we've gotten along well ever since.

Dick's sister was Joan and she had married a local boy named Morris Shaw. The Shaw family owned and operated a dairy milk and ice cream plant. In my opinion, back in the days when I was growing up, Shaw's ice cream was the best ice cream anywhere. Thousands of people still enjoy the brand but it has since changed hands, so I'm not sure if the same creamy smooth recipe has survived.

Aunt Joan was very kind to everyone but I especially felt a warm kindness from her. She had a beautifully memorable smile and a soft gentle voice. I think she treated us Pierson kids especially nice because she knew what we had been through and wanted to make a difference. Uncle Morris was a confident and friendly man. I especially liked how he always referred to me as "Stevearino." It was endearing and I felt special whenever I was in his presence. The family business was successful and afforded the Shaw's a nice lifestyle, but Aunt Joan and Uncle Morris never flaunted it. That said, I fondly remember the baby blue Lincoln Continental car Uncle Morris drove. He always had an air of class about him. The orphanage experience had taught me to read people well; I always read him as a genuine and caring person. I loved his smile too. I miss his smile.

Morris and Joan had four kids: Jeff, Pam, Brian, and Penny. They lived close to us and Jeff was close to my age. Often, I was invited to stay over on a weekend.

I remember Jeff had asthma. It was bad enough that his bedroom, in the summertime, had an air conditioner. Man, those hot nights were never an issue when I was staying there; what a treat. I was always happy when I was at the Shaw residence; everything was wonderful. I felt safe and connected as a family there. I felt the love and the feeling of not having to walk on eggshells. Jeff, Pam, Brian, and Penny treated me like a true cousin. There was no sense of, *Oh, you're a Pierson; you're not really my cousin.* It was never an issue while we were with the Shaw family.

Some of my best memories with the Shaw's include summer birthday celebrations and family Christmas dinners. Often a joint birthday celebration included cousin Brian. His birthday is June 25th and so close to both mine on June 23rd and brother Dan's on June 19th.

Christmastime was the best though. Aunt Joan made the best Christmas pudding; I don't think I will ever forget how yummy her pudding was. Their home was so beautifully decorated. I fondly remember Uncle Morris and his nut crackers. He was always cracking walnuts; but just the way he did it was always a wonderful memory for me. At the Shaw's home, we were all family. I cherish that feeling and warmly embrace those memories.

One of the high points with my Shaw cousins was being able to go to the ice cream plant with Uncle Morris. While he worked in the office, we were allowed to roam about the plant. Being allowed to make our own ice cream cones was so fun. I learned how to swirl a soft ice cream cone to the highest point until it would be so top heavy it would collapse. Talk about being a kid in a candy shop: that would be an understatement.

To say I wasn't envious of my cousins would be false. Not envious in a bad way towards any of them, but I can't begin to count on my fingers and my toes how many times I wished I had been adopted into their family.

Regrettably, Aunt Joan developed an aggressive form of Alzheimers and was hospitalized far too early. I was able to visit her one day while she was in the hospital. It was likely one of the few days left where she had some sense of her memory. I am so grateful for having had that walk with her. I think we both knew her time was running out on our walk, but neither of us mentioned it. I never saw this beautiful woman again until she passed away and I attended her funeral. I can't even imagine how Uncle Morris carried on after his lovely wife was hospitalized. Terrible fate struck him with cancer, not many years later, and he succumbed to his illness and died peacefully with his children around him.

Near the end of his time, I spent an evening with him. My cousin Jeff said his health was deteriorating rapidly, but the day I came to visit, he had so much energy and we shared many laughs. When everyone left, I spent some alone time with him. I was able to thank him personally for how he made me feel special and for his kindness.

I slept terribly that evening thinking about how he didn't deserve this fate. I awoke at 5 AM to head out for work. He was sitting in his chair and gave me a smile. He held out his hand and I grabbed it hard. I didn't want to let it go. No words needed to be spoken. I knew as he sobbed beneath his breath, it was time to go. That was the last time I saw that beautiful man, but I'm grateful for having had the chance to spend his last days with him.

I remain close to my Shaw cousins. They're all married with their own families now, and they're all important to me. We've tried to get together at least once a year. Hosting them at the cottage has been a lot of fun and we've been able to rekindle memories of the past and build new memories together. Adoption was merely a formality. They had and have always treated me as their cousin. I love them for it.

True family is where we live in our hearts. True family allows us to be ourselves, through the best times and the worst times, never relenting in support and love. My true family has always been the Pfeffer's, Verbruggen's, and Cron's. Oddly enough, even the Shaw's as well as Dick's brothers and sister felt more like family than Dick and Gwen did. Sad, but true.

In my latter years, I have reflected upon what kind of parent I would be to an adopted child. Being one myself, I questioned why Dick and Gwen so easily aborted the whole adoption/family thing when things seemed to get more difficult as we reached the teenage years. If I adopted a child, I know I would love and nurture them as if they were my own biological child. I know this because of the relationship I hold with the two children I helped raise in my second marriage. I was fortunate enough to be able to raise Danielle and Amanda; the two daughters of my second wife.

They were aged ten and seven respectively when we began dating. The two girls and I remain very close, to this day, and I have always treated them as though they were my daughters. I would say that they *are* my daughters. We remain in each other's lives and I don't, nor have I ever interfered with the relationship they have with their mother and father. To their children, I am blessed to play the role of grandfather, and we share many happy times together.

If you are reading this book and have ever contemplated adoption; please think it through carefully. Regardless of the circumstance, every adopted child needs to feel loved and be nurtured. I now understand the magical bond between a biological child and their parents, but there must surely be a bond with your adopted child, regardless. And it should be equally as magical, even if in a different way.

Chapter 14

I'm High on Life, Not Drugs

Dick was a *FreeMason* and a *Shriner*. Years later, I became a Mason and a Shriner myself, and this made me question how he could have been so abusive. All the virtues I have learned about FreeMasonry go against the actions of what Dick was doing.

In his role as a Shriner, Dick and Gwen hosted a chicken barbecue and barn dance on the farm, every year. It was a fundraiser. As such, there was a lot of pre-work we had to do. This included whitewashing the stones that lined the long farm laneway, weeding the 200 feet of flower gardens, vacuuming the pool, moving farm implements to the back, and even manually sweeping the asphalt driveway. The driveway was not only long but it encompassed the entire main area around the house and barns. I didn't mind it because I knew all the people coming would see the work I had done. I learned what "pride of ownership" meant from doing those chores.

On one particular evening, it was a glorious sight to see. There were hundreds of cars piled in the back of the farm, and the chicken barbecue pits wafted the smell of roast chickens all day. The spray they used as a basting was a vinegar and butter solution. It was a smooth but tangy flavour. My mouth would water just thinking about getting a sneak taste from one of the cooks; all of whom were Shriners as well. These men I remember were some of the nicest men I ever met in my life. I believe my interest in becoming a FreeMason and Shriner, years later, had a lot to do with the admiration I had for these men.

The dance started after the dinner was served and I still have fond memories of hearing the live band echo throughout the buildings on the farm and all the way up to my bedroom as I would end up going to bed with the window open listening to the music and the soft laughter of the evening.

I should mention that Dick and Gwen installed an inground pool. Having eight kids, this was a smart move, I must say. It was a large pool, measuring twenty feet wide by forty feet long. The deep end was nine and a half feet deep. Working all summer on the farm, the pool was a welcome oasis for cooling down and having fun. I actually enjoyed having to vacuum the pool every week. I found it quite satisfying.

Among my fondest memories of having a pool was when Dick and Gwen's friends would come over for evenings. Many of them would bring their kids for a swim too. I especially remember the Harold and Pat Martyn family. Harold and Pat were wonderful people and I fondly remember Harold, whose nickname was "Turk," after the fact that they were turkey farmers. He was a funny guy and he treated us kids with respect. Their kids included Linda, Ann, Karen, and Paul. They would come over to swim and the night would just go on and on while the parents were playing cards or doing whatever parents do. I doubt she ever really knew, but I held a secret crush on Linda, their eldest. But alas, I think she had eyes for my brother Dan. Of course; he was a jock and a handsome young man, so how could I blame her?

I was an awkward kid, or at least I felt I was, compared to my athletic brother Dan. I was able to play sports but was usually the weakest link on the team. I played hockey early on but was clearly the "ankle burner" on the team. I was self aware enough, however, and never challenged beyond my limitations. But I had passion and heart. This made up for some of my weaknesses.

The only sport I excelled at during high school was soccer. This was because of my senior year soccer coach named Rocco Basacco. He was a math teacher, although I never had him for that subject. That was likely a good thing because I was lousy at math. He must have seen the passion I had for the sport. Well, maybe he didn't, but he took an interest in me and taught me new skills that truly helped me develop into one of the top players on our senior team.

I was voted the MVP (most valuable player) in grade twelve by my teammates. This was an amazing personal accomplishment for me. I learned that MVP didn't necessarily mean the most "skilled" player. This taught me that there was "value" in other skills. And the skills that I had were mostly leadership and communication. Mr. Basacco taught me to be a leader. He built my confidence and my passion. I will always be indebted to him for that.

My leadership skills eventually transferred into school politics. I knew my strengths and weaknesses, so I played to the strengths. I was also funny and could talk my way into a new friendship with ease. I wasn't a threat to anyone. I was likeable and relatable. In grade nine, I was the scrawny kid weighing all of eighty-five pounds, soaking wet.

I tried out for the football team along with my brother Dan. I was politely invited to seriously consider withdrawing, for fear that I might get squashed by a much bigger defensive tackle. I obliged and never went back. Dan, on the other hand, like brother Bill a few years earlier, was an all star in his first year. I wasn't jealous at all. I was happy for him.

With the NFL no longer being an option, I entered into the student activity council as a grade nine class representative. Being elected by my class was a confidence booster and allowed me to get to know more new people. I loved campaigning and had learned to come up with fun and original campaign ideas. I was gaining in popularity; plus, being one of several Barendregt kids in the school helped. Nevertheless, we were teased, by many, as the *Partridge Family* because at one point we had five of us Barendregt kids attending the same high school at the same time.

Having had the experience of public speaking certainly helped me navigate my way through the trials that often surface in a high school environment.

Many of the students in high school were from families that lived inter-city and not out on the farms like we did. It was difficult really getting to know these kids because unless you played sports, or partied on weekends with them, you weren't a part of the "in crowd." Living on the farm and having such strict parents as Dick and Gwen, it wasn't even remotely possible to be allowed to a party on the weekend. We knew better than to ask.

So, I found other ways to gain popularity. I was fast becoming known for getting things done. Students would seek me out to support their causes as a student council rep. I would attack their problems with the same passion I had with anything I did. And I got results. I may not have had real close friends at high school, but I was known well by nearly everyone.

As I said, I was slow on the uptake on finding my stride but by grade eleven, I was not only excelling at soccer, I was definitely in the running to take on the most important campaign of my life at this point: I was going to run for Student Council President. I remember planning my strategy on how to win such a coveted race. I would think about it day and night.

If you, the reader, have reached this point in the book, you won't be surprised in the least at what I'm about to tell you. My excitement at the prospect of running for student body president was just too much not to share. So I shared it with two people. Mother Pfeffer was the first to hear about it. Ken Pfeffer and I were hanging out one day and I don't think I waited a minute to blurt out the news.

"I am going to run for student president." I yammered.

She looked at me with the brightest eyes and the biggest smile and said, "Ah Steve, that's great news and I know you'll win it for sure. Good for you, son."

When I made the same announcement to Gwen Barendregt, she didn't even turn to look at me. She was the second person I told. I shouldn't have bothered.

Instead, she laughed out loud and said, "What? Do you *actually* think you would win?"

She laughed again and then walked away. I didn't care because Mother Pfeffer gave me all the confidence I needed to pursue my goal.

It was clear that some of the lessons I'd learned at a young age in the orphanage, such as learning to survive without parents, were becoming invaluable to me as I was maturing into a young man. Looking back, those lessons made me quite resourceful. I had learned how to observe people. In doing so, I would watch who in the school was popular and determine why this was so. I would use this information to my advantage. Sure, I was popular enough in high school; but I had to ask the hard question: *Was I popular enough to win the Presidential race on my own?*

I had to select a campaign manager for my run to this mighty office of high esteem. So after developing a detailed list of possible managers, I had chosen a winner. It didn't end-up being one winner, however. Instead, I hired three of them.

In my strategic and resourceful way, I thought of convincing the most popular and well-recognized trio in high school, the Ronald brothers.

They were triplets. Tall, good looking, with white blond hair. Everyone knew and liked them. They were the all-star team I would ask to be my campaign managers. I convinced them that if they all worked together, it would be way less work. Hell, I didn't care if they did any work. All I needed was their "celebrity." If the Ronald triplets were supporting "Steve Barendregt For President," then I couldn't lose. I was proud of my prowess.

One of the other candidates was a strong opponent, and I felt that I could very well lose to her. Her campaign manager was my future wife, as irony would have it. We barely knew each other back then.

In the end, I won by a landslide. We were more than 200 votes apart, and I had done it. This next phase for me would be to prove just how effective a leader I could become.

By grade twelve, I was flying high. And that wasn't on drugs either. In fact, some of the most popular students, including the all-star jocks, became my friends. Those who were smoking pot used to tease me because I wouldn't try it. They often teased me to come have a puff with them but even they knew I would never do it.

I dared not, for fear of Dick's wrath. After all, brother Dan was kicked out of the Barendregt home in grade ten for smoking pot.

"I'm high on life, not drugs," was always my slogan and it caught on with even the biggest dope smokers in the school yard. Everyone accepted me for who I was.

Later, someone even said, "We voted for you as president, because we knew you were the only one who wasn't fucked up on dope."

Hey, it worked for me. It was my way of fitting-in without fitting-in.

Every year, the student activity council had a fundraiser to raise money for various things around the school. In the past, we had done chocolate bar campaigns. They did alright, but weren't ever all that successful. As President, I was involved with every aspect of student activity and I loved the empowerment.

One day, I was called to the office. Mr. Howard Branscombe was principal and he liked me, though I never really knew why. I wasn't the kid with high marks. I even confided in him that my math skills weren't that good. I was an average jock. But he must have seen that I had leadership skills and he wanted to work with me on that. He had a practice meeting with all the student body presidents every morning. This was a practice that I enjoyed a lot. It made me feel special. It instilled in me a sense of order and importance.

He was far more aware of my leadership potential than even I was. I learned many things from Mr. Branscombe but most importantly, I learned to believe I had self worth. Because of him, my confidence grew ten-fold that year.

One particular meeting was held to discuss the annual student body fundraiser. He told me the chocolate bar company was asking for a meeting to discuss another fundraiser campaign. Mr. Branscombe coached me that we really needed a successful campaign and he wanted to see that happen this year. I think he knew me well enough, knowing I wouldn't want to disappoint him. I promised him we'd do it.

I can't recall the salesman's name, but he was running me down the rules of how the campaign worked. I stopped him abruptly. I explained that Mr. Branscombe wanted a highly successful campaign this year and I promised to deliver that.

"What can we do differently this year to make that happen?" I asked.

He didn't know, but I was already waiting to pounce on him with my idea.

"How about we offer a large sum of cash prize money for the top three sellers of the chocolate bars?"

We haggled for a while, but, surprisingly, he agreed to my suggestion. First prize would be $750 dollars; second prize, $500 dollars; and third, $250 dollars. This was the most hyped-up campaign ever, and I would suggest perhaps *ever* in the history of the school, to this day. We raised enough money to actually purchase a new vehicle travel van for sports team events. In addition, extra money was made for new sports equipment.

I'd done it! I learned that I had a gift. I believed in myself, knowing that I had the support of others behind me. I learned that I was becoming a good negotiator. I was learning how to effectively communicate, even with adults. My name was inscribed in bronze on the Student President wall plaque and I was proud of it.

I felt that I had made it. I was inspired to do more.

Mr. Branscombe was one of my early influences. When I was going off to college, I confided in him how concerned I was about my math skills. Would I be able to succeed? He empathized with me but encouraged me to not worry; that I had enough skill to overcome any obstacle. His confidence in me bolstered a belief in myself again. I'm happy to report that he was right.

He is long retired, but I am grateful to remain in touch with him and also to have been given the chance to thank him for all he did for me during a very vulnerable time in my life.

Meanwhile, playing soccer throughout all of high school was important to me. Senior soccer was a release. Like brothers Bill and Dan before me, each of us were playing after school sports, primarily as an escape from having to go home any sooner than we had to. Being home just meant that we'd be doing something we didn't want to or getting in trouble for something we weren't aware of.

But like every sport we ever played, or any extracurricular anything, Dick and Gwen weren't supportive. Just like my years in oratorical contests, playing soccer wasn't any different. Neither Dick or Gwen ever attended one game of soccer. Not one. They sure missed out on feeling any sense of pride in us kids as we were developing into fine young adults. Why would they not want to participate? Why not encourage and support their own kids?

Every night after soccer practice or a game in town, I, like Bill and Dan before me, had to walk from the city to the farm. No one was going to make the fifteen minute drive to come pick us up. To walk it though, was nearly twenty kilometers, or about a two hour walk. Needless to say, I was the fittest player on the squad.

That walk also allowed me to think a lot. It gave me a chance to be in my own space, not fearing anyone or anything. I had enough time on those numerous walks to contemplate my future. I also thought about my life. Where was I and where would I go?

I often thought about my mother and mused at the thought of her being able to see me now. Would she be proud? I thought so. I also thought a lot about my siblings who were no longer in my life; especially my oldest brother Gord who was never adopted and was left in the group home in London. I also thought of Bill and Dan. I wondered how Gord felt being all alone, without any of us; especially on the day that we left the orphanage. At least the rest of us were together.

I even thought how grateful I was that Dick and Gwen actually agreed to adopt five of the six of us together. Despite all the other nonsense that went on in the years past, without adopting most of us together, where would we all be now?

I imagined that maybe I would have been adopted into a more loving, inclusive and happy family. That was a welcome thought. But above all, I was grateful to have my siblings together. And at that point, I still had Sandi and Larry living with me.

Dan had been kicked out of the house; but after being away a while was convinced to come back. Dan and I shared a bedroom and it was great for me because I had someone to talk to quite often. We shared our dreams together but we supported each other in times of fear and anger. Sometimes we were so frightened, I can remember that he and I would develop hives from the fear and the anxiety. Dan had it worse than I did, but he likely bore the brunt of being smacked around more than I did.

We would tell and even show Gwen the hives all over our bodies. She refused to offer any help except to tell us to get outside and it would get better. Thinking back, all these years later, Gwen had been a nurse. How could she not know how to treat hives? Her lack of help only annoyed us; and as a result, Dan's hives would just get worse. I felt awful watching him lose his mind from itching. I wonder if she had ever thought of an antihistamine? My God, I wish I knew what that was back then.

I remember a time Dan had had enough and let me know he was going to run away. Like when Bill ran away, I felt sick; actually, more sick this time. Dan and I were very close. Outside our shared bedroom window, on the side of the house, was a TV tower. It was still light out but I can't remember the exact time of day. Dan opened the bedroom window, climbed out onto the tower, and down he went. As I've mentioned, Dan could run fast. He fleeted across the field out onto the road. I watched him for as long as I could.

Then, he was gone. I cried. And I felt afraid; and alone again.

What would happen to him now? All of his hopes and dreams were gone. He was a star football player; popular with the girls in high school, and just an all-round good guy. Despite his all-star capabilities and despite Dick and Gwen knowing full well just how good he was, they never once attended any of his games.

The local newspaper actually had a picture of Dan dressed in his football uniform, pre-game, and holding hands with his girlfriend. It was a sweet picture but the story line said something like, "Star player Dan Barendregt is ready for another big football win." When Dick saw this, he flipped. He chastised Dan about it for days.

He said, "Oh, you think you're a big shot now, do you?"

As a parent today, I would have thought this was about as proud a moment as one could have. This should have been an opportunity to build Dan's confidence and take advantage to enjoy a wonderful moment. But no, not for Dick. It was wrong; dead wrong of him to act the way he did, and Dan suffered long term as a result, in my opinion.

My youngest brother, Larry, was a happy boy. We were two years apart. Once Dan left, he and I grew closer. To this day, we are quite close as brothers and speak at least every week. I misunderstood him, in many ways, until I was older. He was only five years old when Mom died. He didn't have much time to bond with her and certainly, at that age, it was more difficult to develop memories. Years later, when us older siblings would talk about memories, understandably, he wouldn't have any recollections to share. I came to realize just how difficult that must have been for him, growing up. In many ways, the Barendregt family was all he knew. That said, he has always spoken of our mother with love in his heart and I know he would have craved her love and affection every bit as much as the rest of us siblings did.

Larry was the same age as Dick and Gwen's youngest daughter Susan. They got along quite well and supported each other well into their high school years. Like the rest of us boys, Larry played hockey at the local minor hockey league. Larry was a star hockey player early on. Scoring as many as six goals a game wasn't unheard of for him. I remember being very proud of him, knowing just how weak a hockey player I was. His immense skill made it all the more enjoyable to me, really.

Despite Dick's lack of interest in watching his own boys play hockey, he sponsored the local travelling all-star hockey team. They were called "The Barens." With Larry's talent on the ice, the coaches of the Barens team approached Dick to ask if Larry could play on this team. Wow, what an awesome honour for Dick to have his own son on his team, right? Wrong! Here was yet another opportunity for Dick to enjoy what could have been quite an honour as having his own son wearing the Barens' jersey.

But he said, "No."

Dick said he'd refused "because he just wouldn't have the time to take him to the games."

The coaches told Dick that they would happily cover all of Larry's travels. But still, Dick wouldn't hear of it.

Larry's dreams, not to mention his potential to build confidence through the sport of hockey, were gone. Who knows what could have happened if he played on that team? Like Bill, Dan, and now Larry, each one of these young talented men could have, at the very least, been given a scholarship to a university. But none of that happened, and I still ask myself the same question: *Why?*

Despite Dick's lack of support, Larry went about his business. He was a smart student too. He would usually come home with many As and Bs; unlike myself, whose report card usually consisted of some Bs, mostly Cs, and some Ds, for good measure.

Larry and I had a turn at raising farm animals and I will give Dick and Gwen credit for affording this opportunity. This was a great way to learn how to take care of something else, other than yourself. Initially, I had chickens, but Larry demonstrated a lot more patience and passion for chicken raising than I did. Out back, we had a chicken coop. Larry nearly lived there with his chickens, day and night. He fixed up the old coop I had tended to, and I truly believe it was his own getaway; a haven of sorts for him. I have fond memories of him being so happy out there. It was gratifying to watch Larry rubbing his hands together at the progress he made, fixing up or crafting-up another part of the coop. It was always heartwarming to me, to walk out back and hear Larry whistling a tune, all day long. Larry and his chickens, I dare say, are fondly remembered by all of us siblings who grew up on the farm during that time.

But Larry was a bit of a rebel too. The difference though, between Larry as a rebel and perhaps other rebels, was that Larry had a cause. He knew what he wanted and he wasn't afraid to let anyone know. He wasn't as afraid of Dick and Gwen as I had been; perhaps because he was so young when he came to the family and that was all he knew. Or it may have just been because he didn't give a damn. I would guess it's perhaps the latter since that's the way he operates his life now. He has less stress than most people, and I praise him for being like he is.

This is not to say that Larry didn't have issues with Dick and Gwen, because he did. He would often take shit from Dick simply because he would have little to say in the morning. Dick viewed this as Larry having a chip on his shoulder.

I heard so many times from Dick to Larry, "You'd better get that chip off your shoulder before I knock it off."

I'm certain Larry just laughed under his breath, because that's the way he rolled. One day, I was still upstairs in the house when I heard a smash.

In fact, I can still hear the sound. I raced down the stairs and Gwen was standing there.

I yelled, "What the hell is going on here?"

Gwen retorted to me by saying, "Just stay out of this Steve; Larry's learning a lesson."

Really??!!

I rushed past Gwen and found Larry on the ground; shards of glass everywhere. He was bleeding. How the hell was this even a little ok? What in God's name would ever cause Dick to throw his son through a plate glass door? I would soon be off to college and I knew, definitively, that I had to get out of this environment.

But would Larry be safe without me there any longer? That was the million dollar question.

I'm not certain when it all went down, but Dick and Larry had a heart to heart talk after that incident. I will credit both of them for what resulted after their talk. Dick convinced Larry to stay in the house, at least until he finished his grade twelve diploma. Larry agreed, and I know it was the best thing for both of them. But after grade twelve, Larry moved out and came to live with me.

Chapter 15

NURTURING A SEEDLING TEACHES YOU ABOUT LIFE

I had written earlier that going to college was pretty much decided for me. Mike Barendregt had attended (University of Guelph), Ridgetown Campus. This college specialized more in agricultural production management. I was to attend (University of Guelph), Centralia campus. Centralia specialised in agricultural business management. Growing up on the farm, there was no doubt that Mike was well versed in the production aspects of agriculture. Obviously, Dick felt that I had more of a business mind. He wouldn't be wrong about that.

The Barendregt farms were well known in the region as one of the largest flue-cured tobacco producers in North America. Flue-cured tobacco is a type of cigarette tobacco. The term "flue-cured" tobacco refers to the type of curing kiln used to dry, or cure, the tobacco leaves. This takes a fresh "picked" green tobacco leaf off the tobacco stock and then the leaves are hung to dry through a forced hot air furnace and cures the leaves to a golden colour.

I learned much about this process through Dick, for which I must give him credit. He would tell me that I had a "nose" for smelling and knowing when the leaves were cured enough to remove from the kiln. I still love the smell and enjoy that colour of the cured golden yellow or brown of the tobacco leaves.

On the Barendregt farms, we had the latest in curing technology which were flue-cured or air dried curing kilns. There were still many of the old wooden "house" kilns that dotted the landscape around the tobacco region, but that was already "old technology" by then. There was a lot involved in the production of a tobacco crop, and we grew Virginia tobacco. The warmer climate and the sandy, well drained, soil found on the north shore of Lake Erie where we lived was excellent for tobacco production. In Ontario, the "tobacco belt" is a tobacco growing region located in Norfolk County and eastern Elgin County in southwestern Ontario. We lived in Elgin County, where greenhouses were also a big part of tobacco production.

Every year in early April, tobacco seedlings are transplanted into the rich sterile muck of the greenhouses. I always liked this part of the process. We would sterilize the greenhouse seedling beds by applying very high temperature steam. The large square pans would sit over top sections of the greenhouse bed and we would hook up the steam hose and let it sterilize that portion of the bed and move on when it was fully sterilized.

A fun thing for us to do while we waited for the steam to sterilize the soil was to put eggs under the pan. The hot steam made it a perfect environment to hard boil an egg in about three minutes. We always had salt and pepper shakers close by to shake on our eggs.

Tobacco seeds were very delicate and once the greenhouse beds of soil were sterilized, it was important to keep them sterilized. In the greenhouse, all you had to walk on was a narrow walkway through the centre of the greenhouse.

One day, I made the mistake of stepping over the walk and into the sterilized bed.

"GET YOUR FUCKING BOOTS OUT OF THE FUCKING BED, NOW!" Dick yelled all the way from the other end of the hundred-foot greenhouse.

He was pretty far away from me at that point but the use of that swear word meant he was in a foul mood, again. I thought for sure, I was going to get kicked in the butt, or worse, but it never happened, much to my pleasant surprise. I gave a sigh of relief and never made that mistake again.

I share in great detail about tobacco farming here because it's interesting to me and was a fantastic learning experience that I'm grateful for. I might not have realized it at the time, but understanding tobacco farming was similar to understanding Dick's character. I don't excuse his hard or unforgiving ways. I understand now how perhaps he became the way he did. Tobacco farming requires orderly planning, diligent attention to process and has a low margin for error. It requires hours of high stakes, hard work in dust and dirt that can result in an unpredictable yield. When you string a lifetime of days living this way, your spirit can soar or soil.

Tobacco seedlings are meticulously cared for with frequent watering and, of course, require the warm sunshine through the greenhouse glass. I enjoyed watering the plants with the sprayer system in the greenhouse; especially on hot days. Spraying the seedlings allowed me to cool off with the cool mist of the water sprayer. Once the seedlings are ready, they are pulled and transplanted into the field. The time to transplant is after there is no threat of frost; usually in May. Transplanting a six to eight inch delicate plant was an artform.

A transplanter unit is a multi-station frame that attaches to the rear of the tractor. I think ours was a five person unit. Each station has a seat for the transplant person. Each person has a number of freshly picked tobacco plant seedlings in a box in front of them. The object is to set your individual plant on a narrow "table." An arm with finger-like grips would rotate continuously as the tractor moved forward. Once the plant was properly set on the table, the rotary fingers picked-up the plant and carried it through to automatically place it, or transplant the plant into the ground. A rookie mistake would be to place your tobacco plant upside down, exposing the root, when, obviously, it needed to be in the ground. If you weren't quick enough, you would miss placing your plant in the wheel before it came around and no plant would be grabbed and transplanted at all. I made both of these mistakes often enough. If it happened too often, Dick would stop the tractor and just give me that look; the one that was a warning to get it together, or else. This would go on all day. This contraption was a rear extension of the tractor. As a result, there was no escape from the field dust that kicked up in my eyes, throat, skin and everywhere else. Needless to say, I would probably jump on one of those tomorrow, if I had the chance.

Once transplanted, tobacco plants grow in the hot Summer sun. That delicate eight inch plant will grow to a thick stock, about five feet tall, with multiple leaves from bottom to top. The bottom leaves are called "sand" leaves as they're closest to the sand. These leaves are harvested but have less value than the top leaves known as the "tip" leaves. The "tips" are the smallest of all the leaves on the tobacco stock but the most valuable once cured. Tips produce the better valued tobacco. Leaves are harvested based on when they're mature and ready to be picked. Tobacco leaves are picked, starting from the bottom leaves, and then working your way to the top, over several weeks of growing and maturing. It's interesting that the most valuable leaf, the top leaf, is harvested last. As such, as the growing season extends into the end of summer and into the fall, there's a higher risk of losing the chance to harvest the top leaves due to frost.

Like many crops; especially those that grow in well drained sandy soil, tobacco requires ample water. If we didn't receive enough rain, we had to irrigate the tobacco crop. This was a lot of hard work, but also quite fun. A lot of work went into getting set up to start irrigating the crop. We would have to lay the long aluminum pipes throughout the entire length of the field. Each pipe would be hooked together, end to end, to enable the transport of water from the source which, in our case, was a pond at the other end of the farm.

Once the hard work of laying the pipe was done, we would wheel out the large irrigation guns. These guns are similar to your home lawn sprinkler, only much larger. The farm tractor would run the water pump at the pond and then the magic would happen. I used to love putting my ear to the pipes. I can still hear the sound of the water running through the pipes, from the other end of the farm, drawing ever closer to the gun, where I was waiting. Suddenly: phifft, phifft, phifft from the gun, and a powerful gush; then a steady stream of water would rocket out of the gun.

We would have a three-wheel motorbike and a Honda 70 horsepower mini bike. They would transport us up and down the fields as we monitored the flow of the water. Sometimes the pipes would come apart and we would have to quickly find the gap and reconnect the pipes. The power of the water would sometimes wash several tobacco plants out by the time we got to where the disconnect was. Damage repair was required. On a hot day, the irrigation job was always welcomed. Those were fun times.

We were also exposed to caring for farm animals, from time to time. I remember one year when hogs were in high demand on the market, Dick purchased one thousand hogs to fatten-up and market. Every barn, storage shed, or whatever we had were full of hogs. That was a lot of fun and I took quite a liking to the hogs. Years later, I bought some of my own hogs, raised them, and took them to market. Dick even gave me free hog feed from the corn silos he owned. I remember making a tidy little profit. Larry had his chickens and I had my hogs.

In addition to tobacco, Dick grew cash crops. Cash crops are known as a crop produced for its commercial value rather than for use by the grower. In this case, the cash crops consisted of feed corn and soybeans. This is corn that's grown and harvested for animal feed. To support the cash crop operation, we also had a commercial corn dryer operation. This is where warm air is forced through the corn mass by a blower. This takes the moisture out of the corn which is then transported and sold to market. I remember putting together the stainless steel storage bins we used in this operation. It was astounding, the number of self-locking bolts that I encountered in those days.

One thing I disliked a lot was having to go up into the corn silos. Moisture would build up against the silo walls. The corn would become moldy and we had to scrape it off the walls to save the good corn in the silo.

I didn't realize just how dangerous this was until I went to college and learned that the gases from this task could have killed us. The black and green phlegm we would cough-up for days afterwards should have been a warning. And I'm sure that I'm going to pay for that, one day. Nevertheless, the best part of this enterprise was getting free feed for my hogs when I raised them.

I also enjoyed climbing the ladder outside the grain dryer to about one hundred and twenty feet. In the fall, it was especially beautiful being that high up and seeing the wonderful red, gold, orange and yellow leaves everywhere. I felt a sense of calmness up there by myself. I remember feeling the warmth of the sun hitting my face and sometimes it made me feel closer to God.

Chapter 16

FARMING HOPE AND DREAMS

September 1981 was my first year of college, and I was eighteen. I remember the day before leaving for college: I was walking out to the kiln yard where the tobacco was curing. I rather enjoyed doing this with Dick. We made small talk as he opened the doors of the kiln. The smell of the tobacco leaves curing wafted out with a rush of heat from the furnace.

For the very first time in my life, since being with the Barendregt's, Dick grabbed me and hugged me.

He said "You're a very good boy, Steve. Good luck."

I was stunned. I was moved. This had never happened to me and I thought a lot about those words and his actions for many days afterwards.

It was, and is, a fond memory. For such a positively impactful moment, regrettably, his actions in the future would suggest that it was perhaps disingenuous. Honestly, I think it was a rare and beautiful moment. I prefer to remember it that way.

Leaving for college gave me a sense of relief. I no longer had to be exposed to the frequent physical and mental abuse of both Dick and Gwen. But while I was glad to be getting away, the truth is that I really wasn't sure what the hell I was going to this college for. What was I going to do with a degree in agricultural business management?

Dick had always taken pleasure "bragging" at the dinner table on what the bank suggested his net worth was after having had a meeting at the bank. I suppose I was somewhat motivated by this because I had visions of reaching such a lofty goal one day. Perhaps his intentions, although misplaced, may have spurred me to better things.

Dick also used the dinner table to discuss the fact that he owned several farms. I believe he owned at least three of them. He would make us well aware that his three kids, Mike, Cheryl, and Susan, would each inherit a farm. Growing up and being constantly told that I was a Pierson made me never question the reality that I would ever be given a darn thing, let alone inherit a penny.

So, part way through my first year of college, I began to question why I was learning agriculture at all.

It was made perfectly clear to me when Dick exclaimed, "Oh, I'm thinking that when you're done college, you'll come back and work for Mike."

What a devastating feeling.

I remember realizing that very evening, that I was going to college for Dick, and not for myself. Lines were drawn in the sand that evening. Perhaps that was the best thing that could happen for me. In retrospect, I would say it was a realization that I needed to start making decisions for myself and my own well being. This wouldn't happen over night, but it did happen.

I finished my first year that April, but leading up to final exams, admittedly, I was disinterested. I was now, more than ever, unsure of what my future looked like. I had nothing against my adopted brother Mike, but I just didn't see myself working for him either.

By mid-summer when I received my marks, I had failed enough courses that I would have to make up part of that year, if I was to return for the Fall term. I hadn't told Dick; but by that point, I had already decided to take another path. I didn't know where that path would lead but, sure as heck, I knew it wasn't going to be working for him or Mike.

Once Dick learned that I'd failed my semester, he pretty much wrote me off.

At least, I wasn't living at the home farm with him and Gwen any longer. I was fortunate enough to live just outside of town, where Dick owned and operated a farm supply business. There was a house on the property and, with a little fixing up, a great pad for a couple of guys. This is when Ken Pfeffer and I moved-in together. It was a win-win. I didn't want to be at the farm, and I knew that Gwen didn't want me to live with them any longer either.

While rent was pretty much minimal, I needed a job. I had a car that I bought for myself and had insurance to pay. The usual available farm jobs were plentiful. In my search around the neighbourhood, I came upon a new farm, not far from where I had grown up. I drove by and saw a person I assumed was the owner, digging post holes for a new fence. I drove up the laneway.

A new sign with white background and green lettering said, "Hope Stock Farm."

I hopped out of my car and walked up to the man digging post holes. Sweat was pouring off his brow, his glasses were a bit fogged-up from the moisture, and he looked out from over those glasses.

With a big smile and a sigh of relief as if he was praying that I would ask him for a job, he said, "And how are you doing today, young man?"

That was my cue. I had learned how to read a face and understand a situation pretty well over the years.

I don't remember ever answering his question but simply said, "You look like you could use my help right about now."

He held out his hand and introduced himself as Punch Kent.

"I've never met anyone with the name Punch," I stated, after that introduction.

"What? You've never heard of the Punch and Judy show?" as he smiled back at me.

I confessed I had not ever heard of it. He just chuckled and he asked if I was looking for summer work. I let him know I was and that it may even be longer than the summer. Punch decided it was time for a break and he invited me to come up to the house and see what his farm was all about.

Hope Stock Farms was a new farm in our area and one unlike any I had ever worked at. Punch, along with his wife Ann, his brother Richard and his wife, Lise, were building a thoroughbred horse farm operation. Punch was building paddocks for the horses that would be boarded and cared for by him and the Hope Stock Farm team.

I began working for the farm that afternoon.

The immediate need was to build the paddocks. I don't remember how many hours and days or weeks it took, but Punch and I used the power auger running from the tractor PTO shaft endlessly, it seemed. Every now and then we'd hear the grinding of the auger.

"Damn," Punch would say.

We would hit another rock digging the post hole. We sure went through a lot of shear pins that summer.

The greatest part of the job was that the days went quickly. The best part for me was spending all that time with Punch. You really get to know a person when working together for that many hours. We were a team and counted on each other to make the process work effectively.

Punch's stories of his previous life living in the Yukon territories were exciting. I could almost imagine being there as he would describe the northern lights dancing across the skies. It was magical, and I must admit that I still have that on my bucket list of things to do.

Punch was generally a quiet man, but he asked the right questions. In fact, his questions provoked me to think outside the box. I was inspired by the success he had gained at a relatively young age. I believe he was thirty-eight when I first met him. This prompted me to think big and dream bigger.

I fell into a routine at the farm. I was shifting from building the paddocks with Punch to horse management. This of course included mucking stalls; a nice way to say cleaning the horse shit out of the stalls!

As summer came to an end, I had already decided not to go back to college. Punch pushed me to go back. He promised me a job when college was over in the Spring.

When he asked me, "What do you really want to do in life, Steve?"

I answered him honestly: I had no idea anymore. I knew I was not destined to inherit one of Dick's farms, so being a tobacco farmer was out of the question. And I had decided that while I had no personal issue with Mike, working on the farm for Mike was not of interest. I needed more time to think, and staying at Hope Stock Farm allowed me to devise a plan.

The Kent family was always good to me. I especially enjoyed learning more about this world of thoroughbred horse management and racing. Thoroughbred horses are a breed originating from English mares and Arab stallions, when they were bred with native horses to be stronger. I learned the importance of breeding and pedigree within this industry. There were high stakes when it came to breeding the best, fastest, and most durable horses for racing. Richard Kent was particularly involved in this aspect and I tried to learn as much as I could from him.

I knew there was a lot of money involved in this industry. Some of the horses in the barn were worth millions of dollars. This made it all the more important for me to learn how to properly care for them, which included keeping a clean stall, proper nutrition, fitness, and believe it or not, soundness. In short, creating an environment that maintains the horses' overall wellbeing.

One day, Punch informed me that there was going to be a contingent from Greece attending the farm. They were coming to inspect one of the colts who was boarding with us.

I remember Punch asking me, "Have you ever heard of Stavros Niarchos?"

I had indeed. I had read about him earlier. I knew he was a Greek billionaire; a shipping tycoon.

I laughed at Punch, waiting for him to tell me he was joking with me, but he didn't. He went on to explain that Mr. Niarchos, along with a party of possibly a dozen people, would be visiting the following week.

I remember going home that night after work dreaming of how I would present myself to such a tycoon. Perhaps I would have a few words with him and he would invite me into his lavish world of whatever billionaires did. Big ideas and bigger dreams had driven me on more than one occasion before.

The week Niarchos was to arrive, I made sure I took extra care to keep the paddocks cleaned and trimmed. I was extra careful when cleaning the stalls. Everything had to be perfect. And it wasn't Punch telling me to be perfect. I knew instinctively the importance of this. You would have thought this was *my* deal with Niarchos.

Needless to say, I took pride in everything I did, and this has been one of the hallmarks of my success for many years. The day finally arrived. I tucked in my shirt, made sure my pants were clean and neat, and even made sure my shoes were spiffy.

Punch hadn't lied. I still remember Mr. Niarchos walking up the path to the barn to inspect his colt. He was wearing a mossy-green coloured cape over his garments, surveying the land like the billionaire royalty he was.

You knew this gentleman had money and he knew how to wear it. Sure enough, following behind him were about a dozen other faithfuls. What a sight this was.

As he came closer to the barn, where I was, my heart pounded. What would I say to him? How could I make a good impression? *Think Steve, think!* And then it was over. He walked past me with a gentle nod of acknowledgement, and continued on to convene with Punch. I stayed out of the way during the negotiations. After all, I was just the farm hand, right?

What I found so amazing that day was that when Mr. Niarchos was done and ready to leave, he didn't speak at all to tell his entourage that he was ready to go. Instead, he clapped his hands, mildly, three times in the air. No words. Everyone scrambled to take their positions and, with that, he was gone.

If my memory serves me correctly, I think Punch had said the price tag for the colt was about $2.5 million dollars. Debriefing later that day in Punch's office really got me charged up. I don't know if I was driven by money, fame, or fortune, but I realised, once again, that I deserved more than what I was getting in life. I also knew that in order to get more, I needed to put more of myself out there.

I needed to do more.

I had cleaned enough stalls, built enough paddocks, watched foals born and learned much about myself.

I was ready to make a decision. This decision would be for me this time. That was why it was more important. I was finally doing something for me and not someone else.

But before I get to that, I want to share one other story from my days at Hope Stock Farm. As I mentioned, Richard (Punch's brother), was very much involved in the breeding aspect of the industry. When considering a thoroughbred pedigree, among the most important factors to consider are the father and mother's progeny. In other words, what type of offspring are they producing? Good quality thoroughbreds have a well chiseled head on a long neck, high withers, a deep chest, a short back, good hindquarter depth, a lean body and long legs. Richard was always studying these things. He was good at it too, as best as I can remember.

In one instance, Punch and Richard invited me along with them to the horse capital of the world. Yes, this, of course, was Lexington, Kentucky, USA: the home of the Breeders Cup and to over four hundred and fifty horse farms. Reportedly, more money changes hands over the sale of horses in Lexington, Kentucky than any other place in the world. The drive from the farm to Lexington wasn't too exciting, but I was anxious about what Punch told me I would see. "The opulence and the wealth will be like nothing you've ever seen before," he said. As we came upon the steady stream of horse farms, I took in the breathtaking rolling hills along our drive. I marvelled at the horse barns and large entrance gates. The barns were mansion-like in style and in size. I would have happily lived a King's life in any number of those horse barns, I thought.

I especially remember being invited to visit two farms. The first one was Claiborne Farm. This farm was rich in pedigree and famous, of course, for them having one of the most famous race horses of our time: Secretariat. Claiborne has bred, raised, and sired some of the most noteworthy thoroughbreds in history. I couldn't believe my fortune. Here I was standing right in front of the most beautiful stud I had ever seen. He was about as beautiful a creature as one could imagine. And I ain't lying! Some people fall in love with their horses. How could you not fall in love with this beauty? Once seeing him, I understood how he got the name "Big Red." He stood what seemed to be eight feet tall; but, in truth, he was about five feet six inches tall. His reddish coat shimmered, even in the shade from the big tree he was standing beneath.

His tall lean frame showed off every muscle, every vein that flowed the blood through to his heart; that powered such a machine. He was nothing short of what I imagined. I was awestruck.

Secretariat had come to Claiborne farms for breeding purposes. After his racing career at the end of 1973, he stood as stud on this farm until his death in 1989. Claiborne was one of the best breeding operations in the world. I had never seen the practice of collecting horse semen but I assure you, once I saw all these people in white lab coats, I knew it must have been big business. And big business it was. I was up in the stands watching this process unfold. A mare was waiting, so to speak. She was enticing the stallion to come-in and breed.

Two men with long arm-length gloves and a spigit of some sort, wearing lab coats, led the stallion towards the mare. I was absolutely floored when these two gentlemen, and you have to call them gentlemen, began jerking-off the stallion. I think I was the only "rookie" in the stands because no one else was laughing like I was. I quickly composed myself; I didn't want to embarrass Punch and Richard.

Once I learned how expensive a shot of this "liquid gold" costs to breeders, I understood all the science and protocol around it. A gallon of gold-medal-winning semen could easily cost millions of dollars. Imagine, I thought: A million bucks for a shot of semen?

Another memorable moment was learning about and actually seeing the eight thousand acre farm owned and operated by Nelson Bunker Hunt. Punch had told me this gentleman made a fortune in the silver market. I had read, back in the eighties, around the time I was visiting this farm, that Mr. Hunt, along with his brothers, William Herbert Hunt and Lamar Hunt had attempted to corner the silver market. At one point, they drove the price of silver from $11 per ounce to $50 per ounce and turned an estimated profit of between two to four billion dollars. I believe that was short-lived and they filed for bankruptcy a number of years later.

Either way, I was passing through at the right time. Their farm was unbelievable. Nothing was out of place. Guards stood at attention at the front entrance, armed with what appeared to be sub-machine guns. I asked Punch why this was and he smiled and said, "Wait until we get up there and you see the barn. Then you'll know."

I was puzzled but couldn't wait. As we drove up, Punch leaned over and said "What do you think of those barns?" They sure were beautiful, but no more so than the Claiborne farms, I thought. When Punch insisted I look a little more closely at the barn stall bars, I did so. I thought to myself, there's no way that's possible! I looked at Punch, who was grinning, and he said, "Yes. If you're asking, those bars on all the barn stalls are actually silver." You really had to see it to believe it. SILVER FREAKING BARS! HONESTLY?! My thoughts raced back to Mr. Niarchos, his wealth, and his entourage of people. Everyone in this industry must be filthy rich, I thought. Punch was right again. He said I would see wealth and riches like I had never seen. And boy did I ever. It was a whirlwind tour but I learned this was definitely an industry of kings.

Maybe Punch brought me on this trip to show me what was possible in life. Maybe he was enticing me to stay and consider a real career in this industry. I had two thoughts in my head as we headed home. One: Seeing all this wealth, I should be asking for a raise. Two: I definitely wanted more in my life and I decided I would tell Punch I needed to go back to college and finish what I started. I think Punch knew this and I am forever grateful for him showing me a side of the world that allowed me to dream bigger.

I think Punch knew from the moment we met that I was destined to be more than a farm hand. He had shown me a different side of the world sufficiently enough that I knew I wanted more.

Chapter 17

STARTING OVER CAN BE POWERFUL

By the fall of 1983, I was very much on my own. This meant living and paying for everything I needed. I was only now partially connected to Dick and Gwen Barendregt as far as family goes. I was still attending certain family functions, but not really a part of their day-to-day lives.

The closest person in my life was still my best friend Ken. And just like me, he would be off to college a year later. I remained close to the Pfeffer family and attended most of their family functions and get-togethers. They were my family too, as far as I was concerned. I still had a mild connection to my sister Sandi and brother Larry. They too were carving their own path in life, so we had infrequent time together despite still considering them my family. I also had a mild relationship with my adopted siblings, Mike, Cheryl and Susan, but because they were connected to Dick and Gwen, it made connecting awkward. By now, Dick had "decreed" all-things-Pierson, banned.

However, one person I never left, in terms of my relationship, was Gramma Barendregt. I always kept in touch with her and visited often. Near the end of Gramma Barenedregt's life, with her health failing, I received a call from Dick's brother, Brian. Uncle Brian knew how close Gramma and I were.

Over the phone he said, "Steve, Gramma is ready to go I think, but she won't go until she has a visit from you."

I knew he was right. I recounted, in my mind, so many living moments with her. One such beautiful moment connected me to an event that would happen many years later, after I became a father. For years, Gramma spent hours with me as I wrote and delivered my speeches in front of her. She would proudly listen to every word as I stood in front of the picture frame window that looked out towards the home farm while she was in her lounge chair. I had been in this scene many times over the course of five or six years with her. One day, my own daughter, Lindsay, was preparing to deliver her first class speech. Where else would be a better place to bring her but Gramma's home? I explained to Lindsay how, for many years, Gramma B would listen and help me through my speeches. Having won several first place awards, surely Gramma would be the best one for Lindsay to practice her speech with.

Picture this if you will: My daughter Lindsay is about nine years old, standing up in front of the picture window; looking out onto the home farm. Gramma and I are sitting beside each other on her couch, watching my daughter deliver her speech. I was inspired and moved at the sight. At that very moment, it took me back to my days with Gramma. I was so grateful for having her in my life. I don't think I ever loved Gramma more than I did that day. I felt the tears roll from my eyes as I took in the moment.

The drive to visit Gramma for the last time was long and reflective. I think I drove slower than normal because I knew what this visit meant. At this point, Gramma was in a seniors care home. I got to her room but she was curled-up and resting. I called out to her but she was too weak to come around. I rubbed her back. I talked to her.

My thoughts went back to when I used to read the scriptures on Sunday mornings in church. How proudly she would sit and watch me as she sat in her same church pew every Sunday; dead straight ahead of where I stood at the pulpit. At times, when I got to be a better reader, our eyes would lock as I looked up to the congregation. I decided to read her scripture from the bible.

Gramma and I had already discussed me doing her eulogy but we had never decided what scripture she would want me to read.

Starting Over Can Be Powerful

In a loud voice, I told her I was going to read certain passages and when she heard one she would like, she would let me know. Finally, she grunted loudly at one. I took that as being the one she wanted.

After about an hour, her breathing was laboured. I kissed her head one last time and I left. As I was driving back home, not more than an hour into my drive, Uncle Brian called to inform me that Gramma had passed. I thanked him for inviting me to come and see her. We agreed that perhaps that's all she needed was for me to say goodbye.

I did her eulogy like she asked. I put my heart and soul into it because she deserved it. And even though Dick and I were ostensibly estranged from one another at that point, even he couldn't deny the love and the heart that went into her eulogy. When I finished, I folded the written copy in half, walked up to Dick, and I handed it to him to keep. No words needed to be said.

Being "banned" from Dick and Gwen meant no money to attend university. I had dreams of attending Queen's University in Kingston. I was introduced to this university while visiting my girlfriend on a number of occasions. She attended Carleton in Ottawa, but on more than one occasion, we ended up at Queens for some reason. I loved the campus. The architecture and the buzz of the people was electrifying. Paying for everything I needed on my own meant that Queens (or any other university) was unreachable on my budget. I tried several plans to get to Queens but each one ended in disappointment. The fact is, I could have gone to any number of people to ask for financial help. I thought of Dad Pfeffer, Uncle Morris Shaw, and even Punch. I'm certain each would have invested in me. But I just didn't want to ask.

The easiest path and the one that was closest to my own pocketbook was to start over and enroll back into Centralia College campus. I could have waited and started in January as a result of my pre-earned credits, but I said no. I wanted to start all over. When I first attended year one, I was attending because Dick had told me to. I needed to be free of that.

Even though I wasn't certain where a new education would take me, I knew by starting clean over, this time I'd be doing it for myself. I was fully accountable now for my own success.

Starting over is humbling. In my case, it was necessary. Most of the students I had started with initially had since graduated. Other than seeing some of the same deans and professors I had met earlier, it was a sobering reminder of my past failures, juxtaposed against the excitement of what I could control. But this time around, everything came easier. While some of the courses seemed like a refresher, it was mostly my positive attitude that made it easy. Being a bit older and more mature helped too. Some of the courses I found difficult my first time through were now a cinch. I had gained focus. I had big ideas. I had bigger dreams.

Living in residence worked well for me because, other than my residence room, I really didn't have a home. I may as well have been an international student because I lived on campus on weekends and most holidays. I had a car and a room.

I made sure to befriend the kitchen staff. On weekends, with few students hanging around, it was like having my own dining menu available from my newfound friends. The older ladies liked the attention I showered on them and made sure to ask me mid-week what I thought I'd like for dinner Friday night. I admit, I was spoiled. One Friday night I received steak, potatoes, vegetables and for dessert, warm, fresh Baked Alaska. This is a dessert consisting of ice cream and cake topped with browned meringue. Oh my goodness, I had it great until mid-April came, and the college was closed for another summer.

That summer, I applied for a job with the Ministry of Agriculture & Food. I reported out of the Ministry office in London, Ontario, but covered the wide geographical area of Lambton and Middlesex counties. This is a vast area, particularly as an agricultural region. I managed to get through the summer by living with Joy Pfeffer and her husband Mike McCulloch. They had a townhouse in Sarnia which was one of the primary regions I covered for my job. Without this arrangement, I would have been living out of my car again and I am grateful for their love and support then as well as throughout my life.

This role gave me the opportunity to learn new leadership skills. I had to be a leader to the young high school students I was interviewing and hiring.

On what basis was I hiring though? What skills did I have to do that?

All I had at this point of my life was experiences and my gut. It was a wonderful exercise for me from which to learn. In all, I remember focusing on those students who demonstrated a great attitude, were positive, and often those who I felt truly needed the job the most as a result of never having been given a break before.

I still look for these characteristics today as I hire professionals. This experience also afforded me the opportunity to interact with farm owners; men and women who had built a successful agri-business operation. I learned from them too. I learned to carry myself professionally because I felt that was what was important to them. I had to learn to handle crises within a team of young students and problem solve most every week. I had to organize a weekly calendar of jobs and people. It was a great opportunity for me which built my confidence significantly as I went on to prove I was about as good as the Ministry of Agriculture had ever seen. And I remember being told that too at the end of that summer.

The summer went by quickly; and before I knew it, I was moving back into residence. By now, I was determined to work in some form of business but was not yet certain what that would be. Working in the office that summer, I met with many professionals who had jobs that I could see myself doing. What became apparent to me was that most of these people had a university degree. I was enrolled in a university sponsored college diploma program.

When I returned to Centralia that fall I immediately asked for a meeting with one of the student Deans. His name was Don Orth. Don had also been a united church minister previously, I remember. He was a kind man and he should have received more respect than he did from us students.

One main theme I learned from the farm owners with my job as Agricrew Leader was that they all seemed to share their challenges with the banks. Some were more vocal than others, but the frustration they had with the service and assistance from the banks was concerning. I decided, that summer, that I may consider applying to the banks for a job after I graduated. After all, I was learning everything about agri-business management. What better place to apply my skills than a bank; helping farmers? I sensed from working with them that I was likeable. I was a good listener; and most of all, I built trust with the farmers quickly. How did I do that? By delivering what I said I would deliver. I never left them in a bad situation and never had a crew not show-up for work.

I wanted to have this discussion with Don Orth; to get his opinion of the idea. Don had assured me that my leadership skills would truly benefit any bank. He thought I was a pretty sharp lad. However, he made it clear that most banks; especially in the commercial banking world, required university graduates and more than likely the infamous "MBA," Masters of Business Administration. That was sobering to me. He suggested I consider using the credits from college to apply to university, for which it would take less time to finish an undergrad degree. This sounded wonderful but I could barely scrape enough money together for college, which was a fraction of the cost of university. I learned this when I tried to find a way, years earlier, to apply to Queens university in Kingston.

I appreciated Don's candid reality but it just meant I would have to find another way. This was something I had in me from my days in the orphanage. If I needed something and was shut out, I'd have to find another way to get it.

Knowing that I needed to bolster my profile to even think of applying to the bank, I applied for Student Activity Council President. Why not?

I had been successful in high school. The previous year, I had been on the student council and got involved in many of the activities. I was well known by the vast majority of the student body. As I stated earlier, I was a late bloomer; but by this time in my life, all things were beginning to line up for me. Not because they just did, but because I was becoming more aware than ever of myself and my abilities. I also believe I was stronger and took risks because I had nothing to lose. I was cultivating a sense of knowingness. I was a primary player on the men's broomball team. I even made the varsity hockey team, in spite of being the weakest link in my younger hockey years. I wasn't an all-star hockey player but I made the team and I contributed.

I ran for President and came a close second to Wendy. Wendy was a wonderful woman and popular amongst the students. This was a setback for me and I began to imagine how I might leverage my role as VP instead of President on my resume. In the end, I didn't need to do any of that. Wendy failed out of college and I was automatically installed as President; an unfortunate situation for Wendy, but all I could think of was that the universe was providing. I wasn't going to lose time on this opportunity, so I got straight to work; both in my studies and in my role as Student President.

My "triumph" as President was met with a rude awakening after the first semester. Don Orth came to me and sheepishly told me that my tuition was due and if I was unable to pay it, they would have no alternative but to ask me to leave. I had been working on a farm up near the college. Yup - I was shoveling shit again. Only this time it was hog shit instead of horse shit. Don knew my situation. I had essentially been living in residence as my home. I can't remember how much I owed, but it was more than what I had enough funds to cover. God bless this man. Don advised me that he had placed my name into a selection committee for a grant bursary. He wouldn't know the final result for a while, but just knowing he did that for me was heartwarming.

The next few weeks were stressful enough trying to figure out how I was going to get the funds together. Don called to tell me I had won the bursary and that I would receive $900. This was wonderful news, but I needed to find more.

After much thought and deliberation, I called John and Diane Verbruggen. As I mentioned earlier, John and Diane were hard working neighbours close to where I grew-up on the farm. I had occasionally watched their four boys when they went out. I was pretty close to both of them and their family. They gave me the funds to keep me in college with the promise that I would pay them back when I was working.

Knowing the balance of my education was covered, I was able to focus on two important things. 1) ensuring my studies remained decent enough and 2) building a plan of success for myself once I graduated.

I started looking into the possibility of applying to the big banks. I was reminded of what Don Orth had told me but I wanted to focus on the possible, not the impossible. I wasn't prepared to limit myself. Much like when I was that five year old on the front lawn of our rented home, watching the argument between my parents unfold in front of the entire street, I knew I deserved better. After all, I had tried to make a difference by building my leadership profile. President of the college's student council, team sports activity, and community volunteering were all purposefully orchestrated to bolster my resume. What more could I add to that?

I had my sights on possible graduation awards that may add to my resume but I didn't even want to wait until graduation before applying to the banks for a job. I knew my marks were good enough to ensure I would graduate. Waiting until closer to the first of May would put me in competition with all of the other university graduates. Strategically, it made sense for me to get my resume into the bank ahead of the rush. My early days of learning to "survive" while we struggled when Mom was still alive; the orphanage and even at the Barendregt's; they had all contributed to me becoming a strategic thinker.

Starting Over Can Be Powerful

How can I win against the odds? How can I do more, with less?

To this day, I still complete most of my tasks with this in mind. It's an acquired discipline and I always said it was the "fire in my belly" or my competitive nature to win.

With all the confidence I could muster, I built my resume using the help of the college-owned mainframe computer, and researched "How to build a professional resume."

When it was done, I carefully read it over at least a hundred times. I compared it to several more examples of templated resumes through my searches.

I was ready, but I needed a manilla envelope large enough to send it without folding it. I didn't want to ask Don Orth for one for fear he would discourage me from sending it in. So I went to the post office and purchased three envelopes.

Have you ever believed in the value, or the power, of visualization?

People have used visualization to manifest outcomes for years. Others believe it's a mystical or "crazy" approach for "dreamers." Used properly, I happen to believe in the technique as a way of achieving goals. It's helped me many times over the years, and I still use it today. In fact, there are many articles written on the subject, many of which I've studied to develop an ability to use it for my own benefit. This is how I use it:

Usually, I think about a goal I want to achieve. Then, I process the idea for several days; even weeks. Once I have the goal filtered and set to go, I begin to visualize myself in the desired circumstance. I put out thoughts into the universe about my plan and I visualize some more. For best effect, I try to incorporate a number of my senses; this includes sight, hearing, smelling and touch; depending on the complexity of my goal. I use this technique often and I think the more I use it, the more my brain responds to the reality of a desired outcome. Most often, it truly comes to fruition. I've also incorporated meditation to get me started and into the right mindset and/or to keep me focused on the technique of visualization. At times, when I'm distracted, I begin with meditation, which guides me back to my focus.

Visualization helps me to keep my goals realistic. By playing through the various outcomes in my mind, I have been able to filter out what's not necessary in order to achieve my goals and laser focus on what the key elements are to be successful. To some, it's a form of daydreaming. But if you hone your skill, daydreaming often gives way to reality, in my experience.

Visualization has also helped me through painful times in my life. Even though I wasn't aware of it at the time, I was visualizing after my mother died. I used the technique, unknowingly, to help ease the pain and the suffering. I often used it to escape the trauma from emotional abuse, particularly from Dick and Gwen. For example, during the episodes of physical pain, at the hands of Dick and Gwen, I would imagine that I was a boxer in a prize fight who could take a hit and remain standing. When Dick or Gwen chose to humiliate me, I visualized a place in my mind where I was running free in the field, or hiking with Ken in the backwoods. I encourage you to try this to help you achieve your goals. Searching for answers using this wonderful technique may guide you perhaps to consider other positive methods to achieve love, happiness and personal development success.

Chapter 18

CREATING POSSIBILITIES

On a cold evening in March 1985, I placed my resume and a cover letter into one of those envelopes. My confidence was riding high but that didn't stop my heart from pounding. I remember praying as I slipped the envelope into the post box. That was it. I had sent it and now it was up to the "Gods" to make it work. Again, strategically, I only sent my resume to one bank. I decided not to send it to the Royal Bank of Canada since I knew how well Dick Barendregt was known in the bank and I didn't want that to sway my results in any way. In retrospect, it was probably a foolish thought given the hundreds of thousands of clients in that bank, but I was being cautious.

I sent my one and only resume to the Bank of Montreal. Contrary to everything else I'd done until that point, I made that decision quite *un*-strategically. The fact is that I liked their corporate logo. In my opinion, it was clean and crisp: just what I imagined my character would look like if I were to go for an interview.

I continued my studies, and as the warmer weather broke into the month of April, more talk on campus was about finding jobs. I didn't want to tell anyone that I'd applied at the Bank of Montreal, so I secretly panicked every day that I didn't receive a call back from the bank.

By this point, some of my peers were taking interviews. I had even been approached by the Western Canada based conglomerate, Cargill Grains. I was invited to interview for a role with them that would take me out to Saskatchewan. But I slept on it and dreamed bigger. Another week went by. I decided to apply for Cargill Grains if I didn't receive a reply from BMO in a week.

To hedge my chances, I wrote to the bank to ask if my resume had been received. To my amazement, the person at HR confirmed that it had indeed been received and stated that I should be expecting a call very shortly. After that bit of news, you would have thought I landed the job already. I hooted and hollered and danced around when I got back to my room. My heart was pounding again, but this time out of sheer excitement; just dreaming of the possibilities. You see - visualization!

Three days later, the phone call came. The Bank of Montreal wanted me to meet in their downtown Toronto head office. My mind raced. What was I going to wear? No doubt a suit. Did I even have a nice suit? I did, thank goodness. Was I going to be working in downtown Toronto? Hell, I didn't even know how to get to the office. What have I done? All these concerns, but I still couldn't contain my excitement.

The following Wednesday, wearing my grey pinstriped suit, I headed to the "big smoke." I had been downtown to Toronto before, but it was never easy navigating my way through the busy streets. I have always been directionally challenged and the tall office towers made it harder to figure out where I was. More importantly, I definitely couldn't be late. No excuses. According to my map and intel, the drive would take me about two and a half hours. I decided I would leave myself four hours, just to be sure.

I had looked up the address several times earlier to prepare myself for where I needed to be. First Canadian Place. One hundred King Street West, Toronto. I recall my interview was at two o'clock PM. Great, right after lunch. At least the interviewer would be full and attentive, I thought. Was that good? Maybe not, I worried. Was there parking? Damn! I realized part way into my drive to Toronto that I hadn't even checked if they had parking. How would I ever find a parking place in downtown Toronto? I was certain I was doomed. I would be late and then I would lose this opportunity. My nerves were hysterical as I approached the downtown core.

There it was, First Canadian Place. All seventy-two storeys of it.

As I approached the street-level of this magnificent building, I was searching for a parking spot and there it was, a sign that said *underground parking*. Damn, I had just passed the entrance and was too late to dart into the building. I circled back around the block but, this time, I knew where to go. As I wheeled into the underground parking of the tower, I still had forty-five minutes to spare before my appointment. I parked the car, but didn't relax since I still needed to find my ultimate destination.

Within fifteen minutes I had found my way into the common area of First Canadian Place. I still had thirty minutes; the clock was ticking. Feeling less anxious and even a little bit confident, I walked outside, went across the street and down the block, just far enough so that I could take-in the entire building from the street.

I gazed all the way up and dreamed of the possibilities for myself, visualizing the outcome. I must have really looked like a tourist. One of the bystanders on the street chuckled at me and said with a big grin, "First time in the big smoke, is it?" He wasn't all that wrong but I laughed back to him as if to say "Hell no, do I look like I'm lost?"

I made my way back to the concourse of First Canadian Place with twenty minutes to spare. *Time still moving...* I didn't dare enter the main head office branch but I peered in. It was a very large and busy office. Such a place was exactly where I'd envisioned myself working.

With that, I turned and made my way to the elevator. Several people piled-in. I acted as if I had been there several times before so as not to appear like a "newbie." I don't know why I felt compelled to act that way but I think it made me feel more confident. The elevator flew upwards and after a few stops ahead of me the final *ding* was my cue to jump out.

I thought I was gaining some confidence and composure but as I made my way to the receptionist, my heart was pounding so loud that I'm certain the lady at the desk could hear it. My voice broke when I first stated my name. Evidently, my throat was dry. I recovered and confidently stated my name and my appointment with a Mr. Stephen White.

As I sat in the reception area, waiting to be received by Mr. White, I was able to take some deep breaths and slow down my heart rate.

I reminded myself why I was there. I had worked hard and deliberately. I was strategic in my plan and I deserved to be here as much as anyone; with or without an MBA.

I reflected on how proud my mom would be to see me now. That thought brought a calm humility over me. I'm glad, because it helped me be ready for the next moment.

Then I heard, "Steven, it's a pleasure to meet you. Thank you for coming in today."

I don't recall how long the interview lasted, but I remember feeling prepared and confident. I left the interview feeling that I'd landed the job! You know that feeling when you just know you've connected with someone? The feeling had less to do with the right answers and everything to do with connectedness. He said he would be in touch in a couple of weeks. I could wait (but I knew it'd be tough). It would be about seven weeks until my studies were done. And timing is everything, right? I remember thinking that I couldn't have done more to set myself up for success.

Ten days later, I received a call from the bank. They were prepared to start me once my graduation had been verified. They were very pleased to offer me a role as a Commercial Account Manager Trainee. I would start my training in Aylmer, Ontario; a branch close to where I grew up. They wanted me to train in a rural branch because my vocation would focus on the agri-business clients of the bank. I was ecstatic. The offer came with full benefits, a pension plan, and a base salary starting at $23,600. I would start in May of 1985.

"I have the world by the tail now, Mom," I thought.

This wouldn't be the first time I'd drawn energy from my mom to achieve a task. The love I still carried; *had never stopped carrying* from her, buoyed me throughout my childhood and into my adulthood. In fact, it still does. You see, just because someone's physically gone, doesn't mean for a second that they're really gone. Mom's love has always been present for me. In the depths of despair, and especially when I considered driving my car into the lake bank, I ask myself if it's possible that she appeared as Cheryl that day, and saved my life. Thank you Cheryl, and thank you Mom for believing in me. I made it. And I couldn't have done it without you. .

What was even more rewarding to my confidence than the job offer was the call I received from the bank the following week. They were so impressed with my interview and understanding of many of the key aspects of the role, that they wanted to know if the bank could hold interviews for other college graduates at Centralia. They went on to suggest that I might be able to share some names of graduates with them to follow-up with. I felt like a true leader at that point. Not only had I strategically secured myself a role, but I was able to take a leadership role in helping others succeed. How gratifying!

News spread quickly about my success. In fact, the college administration, including Don Orth, were now taking notice. I had created a possibility for graduates. Don Orth was very happy for me and I knew he understood that I had had to take this initiative into my own hands, despite his earlier warnings. As a result, the bank interviewed a few other Centralia candidates. One in particular was Karl VanKlavern, who went on to work for the bank as well.

Graduation day came. I had successfully made the Dean's list with my marks. It didn't hurt that my final genetics exam was a blowout success with a 99% grade. A few of us were studying from prior years' exams as well as from textbooks and notes. I can't recall where the old exam papers came from but they were excellent study templates to say the least. We expected to capture at least a few of the same questions in a current year's exam. But right, wrong or indifferent, when I opened the final exam document, it was exactly, word for word, sequence by sequence, the exact same exam from ten years prior from which we'd been studying.

I felt guilty, to be honest. But, as fate would have it, even though I knew every answer perfectly, I made a mistake on purpose. Call it what you want but I wasn't going to look a gift-horse in the mouth.

I was fortunate to receive a couple of other awards that day at graduation. I received the Minister of Agriculture & Food Leadership Award. I also received the runner-up award for our thesis project that was a year-long group project that covered several segments of agricultural business management. All of us put a lot of time and effort into that project and this meant a great deal to have even been the runner-up award recipient.

There was, however, one point of my graduation that was notable: Dick and Gwen never attended. I was only half expecting them to show.

When I walked up onto the stage to receive my leadership award, I gazed out at the crowd and I realized something: I mattered.

I spotted Mom and Dad Pfeffer in the seats.

I hoped the photographer captured the moment when I noticed them sitting there, because I'm certain my smile grew ten times larger. I hoped they noticed my gratitude at that moment. I don't think I could have loved them anymore than I did that day. Just to be certain, I made mention of them showing up for me that day during my eulogy at Dad Pfeffer's funeral. It was important to me and it still is.

Despite Dick and Gwen not showing-up for my graduation, my adopted sister Cheryl informed me a few years later that Dick had cut out and saved all the pictures from my graduation. There were several pictures of me receiving awards and evidence that I had been President of the college too. He apparently bragged and showed many of his friends and other people the evidence of my college success. But he never once said anything to me about my graduation. To this day, I find that sad for both of us, really. In spite of all the abuse, I would have shared the moment with Dick, him having taught me so much of what I knew about agriculture. Perhaps it was his stubbornness and not a lack of love. I'll never know.

I came to understand, after I graduated, that the bank had returned to the college to interview and hire quality candidates for years afterwards. I really had made a difference. I was proud of that. It taught me that the small efforts of one person can and often do have significant effects on others. I was creating possibilities for others. And I liked that, because it was done without any need for thanks, recognition, or any sort of payback. It was a pay-it-forward act that expressed my gratitude by giving to others as a result of my newfound fortune in life. Perhaps a legacy? If a legacy was not borne with this act, it certainly was a habit-forming characteristic that stayed with me throughout my career and is moreso with me today than ever before. I find more joy and happiness by helping others than I ever thought possible.

A number of years later, with the rationalization of costs and diminishing enrollment, the University of Guelph consolidated Centralia into the other colleges at Ridgetown and Kemptville. And just like that, Centralia was no more. I'm still proud of my time there and what I accomplished personally and for others. It was another time where I had the opportunity to grow myself and put my leadership skills into practice.

Chapter 19

SHEDDING THE PAST

I began my commercial banking career in May 1985. It was a wonderfully exciting time for me. Two years earlier, I had made the decision to start over and that decision was my own. It was the right decision.

My past has been filled with many trials and tribulations. I leaned on some of those events as a crutch over those prior years. But as I embarked on a new career, I was also embarking on *my own* NEW life too. I had shed the burdens of my past with a renewed sense of confidence. At least, I'd done so with regard to my professional life. Though I do make mention of some of my personal challenges later in life, the full complexity of those challenges might have to be examined in book two! But I was no longer the poor little orphan boy. I was no longer young Steven Barendregt who was too afraid to make a move for fear of being emotionally or physically abused by Dick or Gwen.

By giving of myself to whomever or whatever, I was actually getting more for myself from life. It's an amazingly simple concept, but one I had failed to understand until then; a concept I continue to live by today with much success. I was no longer stuck in the ruts that limited my ability to grow.

Going through all that I had from an early age taught me that the goal of life is simple: improve oneself at each level of life.

And what I mean by this is simply that we will be faced with challenges at every level of life. We must learn to overcome those challenges. Once we've mastered one level, it's time to move on to the next. In doing so, this is how we develop a legacy. Always be moving.

I am still mastering levels; one at a time, but I have recognized each challenge sufficiently to understand that each one is unique. These are life's winning strategies. One level at a time, right?!

I poured myself into my new career and established my place within the bank. Rather quickly, I was becoming known for business development. I used my adaptability and my confidence in speaking with others to my advantage. Meeting new clients was easy for me. I realised I didn't have to know everything. I had to be relatable; and most of all, I had to be trusted. I remember my boss at the time remarked how trustworthy I was.

"You have a personality that people trust immediately," he said.

But I have to be clear on this. I never worked at being trustworthy; it was simply a part of who I was and who I am. It's a genuine, almost innocent, characteristic that I'm well aware of but never abuse.

My position at the bank was Commercial Account Manager. Naturally, I had a boss. He was very much a "micro-manager" (I wasn't familiar with that term back then) and made it clear that I wasn't to make any big decisions without his permission.

Each lunch hour I would go for a walk and I would take notice of businesses in town that I knew weren't already clients of the bank. I saw this as an opportunity. After one such "lunch tour," I mentioned to my boss that the local Canadian Tire store was not a client. I felt it would be a great target for me to ask for their business. But I was told, under no uncertain terms, to "leave it alone;" that this was much too complex for me at such an inexperienced stage. I listened.

Several weeks went by. Each time I passed the Canadian Tire store, I became more confident in myself. I played through all the scenarios in my mind (visualizing); until one day, I courageously went-in and confidently asked for the store owner.

When the young lady asked me to wait and that she would check if he was in, my heart pounded.

"Oh my God, she was really going to get the owner?" I thought. *What was I going to say?*

She came back and said, "He'll see you now. Just head up those stairs."

She pointed to a set of long stairs at the back of the store up to a mezzanine level. My legs were shaky and I walked slowly enough to build-up the courage to decide what I was going to say.

In the end, my meeting with the owner and his wife went perfectly.

I couldn't believe it when he said "Wow, your timing couldn't be more impeccable, young man."

I walked out of his office feeling charged-up, but that faded rather quickly, as soon as I realised I had to tell my boss. I'd done exactly what he said *not* to do. But thank goodness, he had to act on my cold call. He didn't really have a choice, now that I'd baited the hook.

His boss was smaller in stature, but a real take-charge kind of guy. I liked him.

At this early stage of my career, I was slightly above a trainee level but was responsible for managing smaller accounts of clients. A few months after this fateful day, I was called into the boardroom by the Vice President who had been visiting. He, along with my boss, our centre boss, and the rest of the commercial team were present.

To my astonishment, the VP presented me with a beautiful leather briefcase with the Bank of Montreal logo as a clasp. He informed me that I was invited to the executive offices to meet the Chairman of the

Board and other executives, where I was awarded the President's Divisional Award of Excellence.

What an incredible three days; so unbelievably memorable for a young upstart like myself.

It turned out that my new client from Canadian Tire was so pleased with how we handled his needs, that I believe he was responsible for convincing ten of his colleagues from other Canadian Tire franchises to move to our bank. As a result, this wave of new store owners developed into what is, today, the Canadian Tire Franchise Finance Program for the Bank of Montreal: my small (and totally unauthorized) claim-to-fame!

Chapter 20

I REALLY DON'T HAVE A NEED FOR ANYONE ELSE

By now, I was developing my craft as a banker. I made the decision that it was time to settle down, get married, and have a family of my own. A year later, at the age of only twenty-three, I was married. Three years later, our first born daughter was appropriately named after my mother, Joyce. Lindsay Joyce Barendregt rocked my world at 12:50 PM, Sunday November 5, 1989.

My life with Dick and Gwen, for the most part, was a distant memory by that point. Those scars of the past were either tucked away, healed, or healing.

I maintained contact with Gramma Barendregt and visited as often as I could. I was also invited to all Barendregt-sponsored events, as long as Dick and Gwen weren't the hosts. I would largely attend out of respect for Gramma. I also had a good relationship and mutual respect with and for my uncles and aunts. Showing up to anything they hosted was always enjoyable. And I was always cordial enough with Dick, but avoided Gwen, mostly.

One Christmas, we all got together. I remember Gwen cornering me in the kitchen. She started small talk, to which I obliged. Then when everyone else had left the room, she asked me the oddest question:

"How have you been able to be so successful when you were such a clutz; a clumsy, awkward, foolish person, as a kid?"

I nearly fell into the old trap of being afraid of what I would say for fear of getting hit. Then I remembered who I was. Towering over her, I leaned down to face her directly.

With a stoic grin-and-bear-it smile and in a whisper I said,

"That is a very good question, Gwen. When I was finally out from under the control and abuse from you and Dick, my life flourished."

Then, I smiled, with true contentment, and without another word, I walked away.

Perhaps because of the dysfunctional relationship that I'd had with Dick and Gwen (and myriad of other reasons which you, the reader, have come to understand), I was keenly aware of my responsibility as a new father. I knew too well what it was like not to have parents and grandparents in my life. I didn't want my daughter to experience what I had.

One day, I visited Dick in his office where he was working off the farm on his farm equipment business. As gut wrenching as it was for me to cower to Dick, I still wanted his approval. If not for me, for my new family.

I told Dick that I felt it was important that we bury whatever hatchets were still being wielded. It was a peace offering. I explained that I wanted my daughter to know him and Gwen as her grandparents.

I told him why this was important to me and how I felt his life could be more blessed with her in his life; even if it hadn't felt that way for me.

I paused and waited for what seemed like several minutes while he just sat there across from me at his desk.

He looked up, smiled a very awkward smile and said, "You know, I have my family. I really don't have a need for anyone else."

I confess, I wanted to cry right then and there, but I didn't. I wouldn't allow him to disgrace me any further.

I stood up, looked him square in the eyes and said, "In my opinion, that is a very poor decision, but it's yours to make."

I knew this would be the last time I'd ever have a chance to speak to him on my own.

I then said to him, "I don't understand you, man. You have an opportunity to fill your life with more people and happiness; to build memories; but you choose not to. I feel sorry for you, Dick, I really do."

With that, I turned and walked out. I don't know for certain, but I suspect that he regretted that decision for the rest of his days.

There's a proverb that says:

> *Cut out negativity, forget gossip, say goodbye to people who don't care. Spend time with people who are always there.*

By saying goodbye to Dick that afternoon, I was saying goodbye to a man I once knew as Dad. I cut out his negativity.

I suppose this is as good a place to share with you my life as a husband. I often joke that I've been married for thirty-six years. It just happens to be that I've had three wives throughout that period.

My first marriage lasted thirteen years to the mother of my two biological children, Lindsay and Matthew. I was twenty-three years old when I was first married. It seemed to me that was the proper thing to do.

I had gone to school, graduated, got a job and felt that it was time to get married. I really didn't have a lot of deep relationships prior to that, except one. I didn't have a steady girlfriend in high school but would always have an informal date for prom and other formal dances. My first sexual encounter was not until I reached the age of eighteen. Like most of my friends in high school, I never admitted that.

I was fortunate enough at that time to get into a relationship that was about as deep as any. She was a university student who worked for Dick in the summer on our farm. She rode a motorbike which was a turn-on as far as I was concerned. Much to the misplaced judgment of Dick and Gwen, I started dating "Dee Dee." She was the best thing that happened to me because she taught me a lot about adult relationships; something that was necessary for me because of my lack of experience. Our break up was hard on me (and on her too, I'm sure), which triggered my feelings of abandonment all over again. The sense of abandonment I harboured wasn't her fault; that was on me. It's the way I instinctively reacted to the break-up.

My first marriage was blissful, I would say, for the first six or seven years. My wife, at the time, worked shift work in a hospital which wasn't an issue until our first child Lindsay came along in 1989.

With shift work, I often felt like a single dad. There were wonderful times though, in which I had Lindsay all to myself. We would spend countless hours just getting to know one another in those first few years.

I was busy working at the bank and Lindsay's mom was busy at her hospital job. Shift work meant that we would pass each other in our comings and goings; without much time to talk about anything other than Lindsay. And so, our own needs were suffering. I sensed, at the time, that her life had become much more stressful, and her shift workers were more like her family than I was. Usually after a midnight shift she and her co-workers would catch the last call for a drink which was never an issue to me until we had our daughter. These "one-drink-and-home-in-an-hour" episodes started turning into three and four hour sessions.

Without realizing it, my sense of trust and abandonment issues surfaced again. I began to be suspicious of everything and everybody. I started building walls and pushing my wife away as a means to protect myself from what I expected was her desire to abandon me.

I can see now that I had subconsciously been doing this throughout my life, ever since Mom had died. I had internalized Mom's death as abandonment, without ever knowing it. Eventually, I took a transfer with my employer and we moved away from the city in which we were both working. We thought by moving, that our issues would improve.

Meanwhile, we'd been trying for another child without early success. Then in 1994, our son Matthew was born. This was certainly a joyous time for all of us. Lindsay became the big sister with a five year age gap, and she certainly took advantage of her new role.

We seemed to get ourselves back into a family groove but that nagging sense of mistrust and abandonment wouldn't leave. In 1999, we separated.

The children's mother and I were star divorcee's though. We co-parented extremely well through all of our children's formidable years, attended school functions together, and for even a few years afterwards, friends still weren't aware that we had separated. I'm grateful that we remain friends to this day. We celebrate and still work together with our children and now grandchildren. She is a very giving and loving mother.

My second marriage brought me two wonderful step-daughters, Danielle and Amanda. When I first came into their lives they were ten and eight, respectively. I had met their mother through the glass of my boardroom office. At the time, my business was flourishing and we rented part of the office to a divorce lawyer we knew. One day, an attractive young woman arrived for a meeting with her lawyer. I introduced myself purposefully and advised that I'd go fetch her lawyer from her office for their scheduled meeting.

I must confess that I set my chair up in such a way that I could see this young lady in her meeting. Not very professional of me, but I didn't say I was perfect. Of course, if she was in the lawyer's office, she must have been getting a divorce, I figured. And as unprofessional as it was, I just had to find out her name. Eventually, I tracked her down and asked her for a date.

Having a blended family provided a new set of challenges, but we worked it out. We moved into my home and Lindsay and Matt stayed with us every other weekend. The kids all got along well and we were pleased. Four years later, with prodding by the kids, we were married. I was busy building my company and she was working at a bank with a budding career too. I was as much in love with the two girls as I was to her family. Her father was a legend in his own right, having had an illustrious career; but I loved him for the simple and giving way he had about him. I wished I had learned more from him.

I can't pinpoint exactly when things started getting worse in my relationship, but my sense of abandonment flared its ugly head again. I became suspicious and non-trusting again.

As I look back on our ten years together, I was figuratively smothering her. I questioned everywhere she went and everything she was doing. I was unable to come to terms with this sense of abandonment that had followed me my entire life. I felt, rightly or wrongly, that she'd lost the love and respect she had for me. I couldn't help myself from building that wall up and protecting myself; all over again.

With two failed marriages, I needed to reevaluate myself.

For the first time, I began to look deeply into what was causing me to feel so abandoned that I would sabotage my relationships. But regardless of what I was to discover, by the time I was married to my present wife; I had come to realize that I had to make some significant changes in my life. I knew that in order for me to have a deep relationship, I needed to know and love myself. Because what I knew for certain is that I loved the whole concept and notion of love, marriage, and family.

I realized in my first marriage that I was young and inexperienced in the world of adult relationships. I needed to work out a lot of things if a marriage was going to be sustained. I didn't do that then; I didn't know how. And even before being able to work on my marriage, I would have to come to terms with the scarring that had built-up over a lifetime of trauma in the form of abuse and the misconceptions I carried around with me. I was attached to the idea of marriage because it was the "next natural thing to do."

In my second marriage, I realized I'd selected a step-mother for my children instead of a lover and life partner. I expected her to absolutely love my children without question. That wasn't fair. She barely knew them since they only stayed with us every other weekend, for the most part. I placed my children ahead of my second wife at all costs, perhaps because I'd been neglected for so long, in my past. I was overcompensating. While I didn't see it then, it's as clear as day to me now. Regrettably, the result is that I'd built a moat around myself; impenetrable by even my wife. I'm so very grateful that my relationship with both Danielle and Amanda has only blossomed. I am blessed to have them, and now their own family and children, in my life.

I am deeply in love with my present wife, Sandra. I feel supported in every way. Oddly, I feel spoiled and undeserving sometimes of just how much she cares and loves me. Perhaps that's a reflection of loving myself in a healthier way than I have in my past. I feel as though I can give back in a much better way than I had been able to before.

When I met Sandra, she had a successful career and owned her own home. She had never been married and had no children. What a catch for a 45 year old twice-divorced person, right?

Upon meeting Sandra, this is what I told her: "I have been married and divorced twice. I have two children; Lindsay and Matthew."

I went on to say that I had two other kids; albeit not my own, biologically. They were from my second marriage, but I loved them nevertheless and they had to be a part of my life.

I knew I'd met a wonderful person when she smiled a bewildered smile and said:

"That's fine with me."

Sandra completes me with her humour, her understanding, and her warm heart and soul. Most beautifully, she loves my children, including Danielle and Amanda, and I know that she's been as enriched as I have with our four children and their children.

As life continued its forward moving momentum, I emulated its progress by attempting to give more, which only created more fulfillment in my life. I was involving myself in areas other than just my work at the bank. I joined industry boards that afforded me the opportunity to build my profile and be introduced to new spheres of influence. I was getting involved in community charity work which fulfilled my need to give back. At the same time, I was also able to help others who were less fortunate. I'd never forgotten where I came from. I never forgot the struggles my mother went through to raise six children on her own. I wanted to get involved with charities that helped people like my mom and our family, and so I did.

It's really a simple law: giving attracts getting. Through my outside of work volunteering, I was introduced to influencers within the business community. As a result, in 1991, I was invited to apply for a scholarship. It was for a group study exchange sponsored by the International Rotary. They would be selecting five young professionals to participate in an exchange to Germany. After an interview process, I was selected along with two other young men from Ontario and two from the USA. We formed a team who would represent North America. We would be Ambassadors to foster goodwill and learn about our respective vocations. Ironically, I was billeted with five different families over the course of five weeks. I mused at the thought of being billeted to these various families. It reminded me of my days as a foster child.

I Really Don't Have a Need For Anyone Else

But this was an opportunity for me to learn about the culture and how businesses operated in Germany. The gentlemen, all Rotarians, were highly influential. Three of the five families I stayed with were Chairmen of their respective banks. Interestingly, I didn't learn a ton about how the banks operated in Germany, but I suppose that wasn't the primary objective. Instead, I learned about people who were proud on the one hand and ashamed of their past on the other, particulary as it related to Hitler and the holocaust.

In the process, I learned a lot about myself. Traveling across Germany allowed me to reflect upon my life. I was learning to appreciate all that I had done to elevate myself from whence I came.

I was also beginning to realize that I wasn't alone. No matter where you travel in the world, people deal with the same types of traumas, the same levels of guilt and shame that we do, here in North America. I became increasingly proud of myself. I knew my mother would be proud too and that brought me a sense of happiness. I was succeeding at almost everything I was doing at this stage of my life. It was becoming quite apparent to me that while luck played a role in my triumphs, planned strategy, perseverance, and confidence played an even more sustainable role.

I was developing a winning formula for life success and, yet, it was all for self preservation, growth, and esteem. I hadn't yet fully recognized that I had a gift to share with others.

I have always had an interest in other people and have always wanted to help wherever I could. But I certainly wasn't ready to be an effective coach or a mentor. How could I be a mentor without more experience to draw from? As such, I continued to be open to new opportunities with a view to learning more. One day, that would allow me to help others.

What I probably hadn't realized was that I was helping. In spite of limited work experience, I was helping people all the time - helping customers, helping the corporation recruit exceptional candidates, and helping my family. No doubt, I still had a lot to learn, but I was helping.

By 1994, I had achieved an exciting position as Vice President, Commercial Services for a smaller trust company. I was actually hand-selected through the trust company's centres of influence. They felt that I had what it took for the role. It's always a nice position to be in when an employer is looking for *you*. It certainly takes a lot of the pressure off. At this point, the trust act changed to allow trust companies to lend within the commercial business sector, where once they were restricted by regulators. What a great opportunity to be on the ground floor of something new and exciting.

As I prepared for the interview process to land this new role, I evaluated myself. I was really looking inward and asking myself, "Are you sure you're ready for this role?"

Again, what pushed me to get out of my comfort zone was a continued belief that I deserved better. As I'd done my entire life, I had to make this work. It was the experience I needed to develop and grow into a leader. I felt that I had the sales skills, but lacked the experience in corporate governance and senior leadership. Given that this would be an entirely new lending program within the trust company that required policies and procedures to be built-in, this would fall under my purview. In my past, I'd always had policies and procedures to follow but actually creating policies was unexpected. To be honest, if they had asked me in the interview process if I had this experience, I would have had to say no.

I believe what they were looking for, above anything, was a "go-getter;" someone they felt confident could build something from scratch. I was known for strong negotiation skills and an ability to get things done.

My preliminary interview went well with the head of HR and the President. However, I had to have one further interview with the Chairman of the Board. While the trust company was publicly traded, the Chairman and Founder pretty much owned full control of the trust company.

I had heard stories about Mr. Max Rotstein but didn't pay too much attention to them. From all accounts, he was a ruthless man. I was told that he would eat people up and spit them out for breakfast. Rumour had it, his wife was even more ferocious.

The interview with Max Rotstein is worth sharing. I was invited to drive down to Toronto to meet with him in one of the hotel properties he owned. When I arrived, I was instructed to wait in the meeting room until Mr. Rotstein showed-up.

After the first ten minutes of waiting, I was growing uneasy.

Had he decided not to bother hiring me?

But I remained calm and cool and maintained my composure. After twenty minutes of waiting, I decided to grab some water that was placed on the table. I was beginning to expect that he might be watching me through some hidden camera, just to see me stir. It wouldn't be unlikely from the stories I'd heard.

Then, as thirty minutes went by, I decided I wouldn't implode with anger; but rather, I would use his tardiness to my advantage. I reminded myself that I already had a good job and really didn't need a new job; as much as I wanted this one. I was building more confidence rather than sinking into depression and anxiety over his being late.

I decided I would give him five more minutes. Then, I would walk out if he didn't show-up.

Whether he had a camera watching or not, I will never know, but within two minutes of my internal five-minute countdown, Max Rotstein walked-in.

He didn't even come to shake my hand; but rather, walked-in, went straight over to the window and announced what a beautiful sunny day it was. I didn't say a word and decided it was best to let this man play out whatever he wanted to accomplish. It was a good decision. It allowed me to size him up as he spoke and moved without any of my engagement. He was the one who was now uneasy and I knew I had him exactly where I wanted him.

He turned, offered a big smile, sparkling eyes behind his black framed glasses and said, "Welcome Steven. I apologize for holding you up."

I replied, "Thank you for your apology. I was just about to leave the interview, had it taken a few minutes longer."

And, with that, Max Rotstein and I cemented a bond of mutual understanding, I think.

I'd remembered hearing that Max would run you over like a train if you let him. He apparently didn't like "weak" people. So, I decided to play his game. When I very matter-of-factly advised him that I already had a good job and didn't need this job, it had to be music to his ears.

I wouldn't recommend this tactic at all unless you want to find yourself in the lobby as quickly as you came in. But you have to know your audience; especially in a job interview. For me, the standard practice before any interview is to research and have at least some general knowledge of the company's:

- Products & services
- Mission statement
- Value proposition offering
- Markets served
- Competition
- People

And most importantly; if you can, know something about your interviewer.

I Really Don't Have a Need For Anyone Else

Before long, I knew I was the right man for this job. And after the interview, just like I recalled years earlier at my first job interview with BMO, I had the job. It was just a matter of waiting for them to call me back and make the offer. It wasn't arrogance; it was confidence in the ability I had in reading the room and the person in Max Rotstein.

Max and I got along well because I knew all he wanted was results. I went out of my way to deliver results quickly. We met often and I learned a great deal from him about the business of banking. I especially learned that small town Ontario, which was his primary market, was widely underserved by other financial institutions except by the big banks and, of course, by Max's company known as Municipal Trust.

Stay with me here, as I share a great story from my short time with Max.

After my first year, the new commercial lending portfolio was going quite well. I was earning a good base salary but also good quarterly bonuses based on performance. One day Max called me into his office and offered me the role of Senior Vice President, Real Estate. Max went on to tell me this job came with a better remuneration package and that I was to go out and buy a new car which was a perk of the new job. I wasn't entirely confident I had all the skills to take this new role on but I wasn't about to let Max know that and I accepted the job right away.

With that, he instructed me to get out and buy that new car, which is precisely what I did. I was thirty-three years old and a Senior Vice President of a financial institution. My confidence grew along with my realization that I had a gift of building trust with even the most influential people in my world.

A facsimile went from Mr. Rotstein's office to the entire company of my new promotion. I don't think it was even twenty minutes later that the President entered my office. I was preparing for him to congratulate me. Instead, he asked me who had promoted me to SVP. I was stunned, because he was visibly upset. It turns out that Max, as he always did, made decisions without notifying the board; and even more surprisingly, without notifying the President.

Two weeks into my job, I was visited by one of the board directors. I knew this gentleman through my association in FreeMasonry. I think they sent him in to talk to me because we were familiar with one another.

He confided in me that my appointment was a real *fly-in-the-ointment* since the board was working on a plan to sell the company to a larger bank; unbeknownst to even Max. My executive appointment would cause great concern with the negotiations. The result is that he asked me to step down. The challenge was that my former role had already been filled, and I was effectively without a job.

Naturally, I sought legal counsel. My lawyer advised me that I could win hands down as this was about as good a constructive dismissal case as he'd ever seen. I was looking at a hefty settlement, he said.

I evaluated the situation.

Rather than take advantage of a short term win, I saw the long term opportunity.

I had learned in my short time in this role that small town Ontario businesses had few alternatives to the big banks. Knowing my days in this role, even with the new bank owner would be numbered, I once again found myself thinking big and dreaming bigger.

Could I actually start my own company?

Did I have enough experience to succeed?

I suggested to the President that rather than taking the issue to court, why not allow me to stay on three more months? In that time, I would develop a business plan to start my own business. I knew my strengths but, more importantly, I knew my weakness, which was working out the administrative details and managing the legal-ease required to operate an equipment lease origination business. The good news was that I found a solution by engaging a smart and talented young lawyer who was also working for the Trust company.

Thus, we began as business partners. He had previous corporate Bay Street chops, combined with bank finance experience as a lawyer. He was quiet and reserved and his attention to detail was far greater than mine. We were polar opposites. I knew this would work well.

Three months later, I was walking out of my office from Municipal Trust with a bankers box filled with a few personal items, but armed with a whole lot more confidence and focus.

Despite being in this pivotal role for only a couple years, I learned a lot of important lessons:

- Don't sell yourself short with opportunity just because you don't have all the qualifications listed in the job outline
- You can learn and adapt and excel in any environment with a positive attitude
- Learn about the centres of influence within the company as quickly as you can
- Build your own impression of someone, not through the rumour mill
- Sometimes your adversaries, in the beginning, become your best allies when it counts.
- Find one sliver of goodness in every person and work with that to build trust
- Policy and procedures are difficult to develop and it sucks if you're sales-oriented

Walking away from that job to strike out on my own was truly invigorating. It was also a tangible reminder of the knowledge I had, being a banker for several years, on how often new businesses fail.

Chapter 21

BE BRAVE AND CREATE

Relying on other people to start my first company was a humbling experience. I had built a business plan to set out the scope of the products and services we would provide. I had not put much thought into our office facilities, telephony and other office needs.

A friend and local business entrepreneur, Jerry Rose, was very generous in giving me a spare office and business phone in his office building for free. I settled nicely into Jerry's office and got to work right away in building out the plan. Being able to generate sales leads was easy for me. Running and tracking administrative tasks was another. Thankfully, it wasn't long before my new business partner had orchestrated his own exit as in-house legal counsel for Municipal Trust that he joined me.

We needed to raise some start-up capital before we were able to generate sufficient sales to carry the business on its own. We issued an Offering Memorandum to potential investors to invest in our plan. Ultimately, they were really investing in us as individuals. Before long, we raised sufficient working capital through local business contacts, friends and family; promising a good rate of return for their investment. Having my lawyer/business partner craft-up these agreements was invaluable.

One of our new investors owned office premises and we decided it was a good business move for us to take up space with him. We left the free office space from Jerry Rose but we made sure to thank him in style. Every year for at least a few years, I would buy him a stylish Hugo Boss shirt. It was a nice gesture and a whole lot less than what rent would have been. I always pay Jerry credit for getting me started in my first venture. We remain friends to this day.

My business partnership was a good mix of polar opposites. My lawyer partner took care of the administration and legal details of the agreements and I was 100% the sales and marketing team.

You learn a lot about yourself when you're in a working "eat-what-you-kill" environment. Anyone who's on a commission-only remuneration platform, or most entrepreneurs, know full well what this means. This is where your paycheck is solely dependent on you and your ability to produce, and more importantly, close a successful transaction.

I was in the money-lending game when I started my first company. Everybody wants money, right? That may be mostly true, but I was competing with the big banks and other financial institutions that had much more buying power than my little start-up. From my experience working in the role at Municipal Trust, I learned that small town Ontario businesses really only had the big banks to do business with. I felt there may be a niche to offer competitive financing but with significantly less red tape and much more customer "white glove" service.

Here's some of what I learned from being a first-time entrepreneur in an eat-what-you-kill environment:

- Make sure you have some sort of financial safety net to withstand the lag between starting out with no revenue until you've generated a reasonably steady stream of revenue. This will last from three months to twelve months; so keep that in mind.
- Connect with people. It's important to understand who your centres of influence are. They are a built-in sales force that you don't have to pay. What you owe these people is your integrity. Through your success, you'll make them look good too.
- Understand your product and the differentiator you have that sets you apart from your competition. Know this before you start and hone it as you develop yourself and your company.

- Be brave. Don't sit in your office and wait for the phone to ring; it won't. At least until you have built a market reputation.
- Be creative. You have to learn to identify every possible avenue in order to offer a solution to any problem your client may bring you. I made a point of asking many questions which often led to more opportunities for me to introduce a solution. That turns into much needed revenue; especially in the early days.
- Offer free advice as often as possible. This builds trust and loyalty. But be careful to ensure that you're not being taken advantage of. Some will take (and take) your services. You have to only give them enough free advice to prove your value proposition.
- Be patient when you're "eating what you kill." Make a point of being efficient and effective, quickly. Time is really money in this case.
- When you're successful with a client, ask them for a referral. There is no better way to develop new clients than from a satisfied customer.

I remember being asked in an interview years before: *What is your greatest accomplishment?* I mention this at this point of the book because it invoked so many emotions that carried me into what was going to help me survive the challenges of starting a new business venture.

I want everyone to really think about that question. Most of us automatically go to that corner of our brain that suggests my degree, my championship trophy, my marriage, kids, and such things.

I wasn't even prepared for such a question when I was first asked, but I think my greatest accomplishment may very well be my response to that question.

The interviewer had her head down, looking at her page when I responded.

"My greatest accomplishment has been failure."

The interviewer shot her head up so fast she may well have gotten whiplash. She was pretty stunned, to say the least.

I went on to tell her that because of my failures I had become stronger. Failure has forced me to evaluate my processes and find better, more sustainable solutions.

Failure has taught me that it's ok to fail and that it doesn't have to hold you back. Failure teaches us to be humble and empathetic and know there's another way to get something done that may not be our way. It teaches us that we don't know everything. Learning is continuous and required for self development.

I knew I had the interviewer's attention when I said all these things as she was feverishly writing my comments down with great speed. I knew it was something she may not have ever heard before. But I held the real zinger to the end.

I said, "My greatest accomplishment is yet to come. And I hope this interview will be the start of that for me today."

This was not a lesson I had been taught, or ever discussed with anyone before. It stems from the realization that we all have a gift and a power. I believed this well before I started my first company. I had built some experience working several years in a financial institution. I had gotten out of my comfort zone a few times and I succeeded.

It's important for us to recognize our inner power that drives us not just to survive, but to succeed. Because we all have a survival instinct; it's the success instinct that simply needs to be recognized. And that happens when we believe in ourselves.

Failure is often only someone else's opinion of what you're trying to do. Use the criticism to reassess and drive forward; sometimes changing direction. It's more important to keep your focus.

The point I'm making here is that we often go through life without realizing or understanding *why* we are faced with certain dilemmas or difficulties. That interview, years before starting my first company, set me up to understand what I was heading into and to face what I was heading into without fear.

Those difficulties I experienced as a child: losing my mom, living without a dad, living in the orphanage, growing-up in an emotionally abusive adopted family environment – all these challenges actually *improved* my life in so many ways. I learned these lessons at an early age, but I understood them better as I aged. I came to understand that difficult times will come but they seldom last. If we learn to overcome our failures and see growth in ourselves, we'll do more than survive: we'll succeed.

And succeeded, I did. I'd become President of the student council in high school. I'd succeeded as an orator. I even gained valuable leadership skills by reading the scriptures every Sunday at church. That experience extended to my time as President of the student activity council in college. Most of these experiences were self fulfilling. But while I was learning certain aspects of leadership and accountability, I was still only taking care of my own needs. Nothing would prepare me for the type of leadership in which I was truly responsible for others. I didn't really understand that other people's success meant my own success.

All the previous years for me had been performance-based leadership. If I succeeded, I gained. True leadership is letting go of ourselves and focusing on others.

While in certain cases of my life journey I had others in mind, I realized that most of my decisions were what was best for me and not what was best for others. In fact, much of what I was doing to succeed was at the expense of others; not intentionally, but that was a sobering realization that caused me a degree of self-loathing for a time. I am reminded of those words I first heard from Wade Stayzer; a colleague of mine at Meridian Credit Union: **"Leadership is a tough business."**

Leadership isn't about *you*. Rather, it's about others. In my capacity as an Owner/Leader, that was a difficult adjustment because I was always the "deal-doer." I had to learn to be the coach and the mentor; allowing others to grow and build their own experiences.

As a coach and mentor, you have a significant responsibility to those to whom you are entrusted. I take this seriously. It's incumbent upon you, as a coach and mentor, to be inspirational.

I found it quite a challenge throughout COVID-19 to keep my team of about twenty-five talented young professionals motivated. As a leader, I knew I had to be passionate first, in order to create a culture that inspired my team. I communicated far more regularly to the team as a whole; but more importantly, to each person individually.

You must be vulnerable in order to build trust. I coach that to my senior leaders often. I made myself vulnerable and it's something I've done for years not only with my team but with clients too. By doing this, we become more relatable.

Through the COVID pandemic, I tried an experiment with my team. I genuinely empathized with each of them, trying to navigate through an environment that none of us had ever experienced. As such, I arranged a virtual audio/video call. (Side note: I make a point of insisting, when I'm on a video call, that both parties turn on their camera. I'm perplexed how some people can actually join a two-person video call and *not* turn-on their camera. It's a resounding *slap-in-the-face* to the other party, in my view.)

In any event, once we started the video meeting I asked the question, "How are YOU doing today?"

In every case, on every individual call, I received a similar answer: "Well, I'm keeping busy with work on my desk and issues I need to attend to for clients."

In every case, I stopped the conversation and politely interrupted to say, "I'm not asking about your work. I'm asking how YOU are doing. So how are YOU and YOUR FAMILY doing through COVID-19?"

It was amazing to me to see their reactions. They were taken aback. How often do we truly step back and ask a simple question with such genuine and heartfelt passion? We don't do it enough as leaders.

That exercise was very emotional for me, as well as for my team. Once the individual realized what I was truly asking, their eyes lit up, a smile came to their faces, and everything became personal and real. I had some shared tears and, above all, each one of my team members thanked me for caring. I encourage every one of you to consider this. You don't have to be the titled leader. I always coach that, *when it strikes you to care; don't wait to share. Do it and change someone's day for the better.*

As a coach and leader, I've learned to communicate early and often. I think that's one of the most important actions any leader can choose. But it's equally as important to understand that too much communication can also be taken as micromanagement. I detest micromanagement. It strangles creativity and eliminates confidence. Don't be a micromanager.

It's an amazing feeling when, as a leader, you know that you've contributed to the creation of another leader. I coach to the very real idea that you don't need a title to be a leader. In early 2022, from various books I've read or quotes I'd come across over the years, I crafted up a creed for the team to follow.

Here's what I shared:

> *YOU are a LEADER; no matter what you are doing because in everything YOU do, YOU have the ability to INFLUENCE.*
>
> *As an effective LEADER, YOU want to articulate a VISION; a common objective that MOTIVATES and involves TEAMS to ACHIEVE organizational goals and promotes a healthy organizational CULTURE.*

As an effective LEADER, YOU support your employees as well as your teammates and help them GROW.

In addition, effective LEADERS set a direction with their teams and give them a means to ACHIEVE objectives and overcome challenges.

Effective LEADERSHIP is something dynamic; a whole that is based on a variety of characteristics that establish clear lines of RESPONSIBILITY and ACCOUNTABILITY; all of which hinge on the personality of the LEADER.

Being a LEADER is not a function or an official title, but a set of behaviors and a charisma; which, in the end, invites everyone to want to listen to and surpass themselves.

An effective LEADER does more than efficiently manage team members to complete their missions at a high level of performance and efficiency;

YOU as LEADER must go well beyond these functions.

So, are YOU leading effectively?

If not, it's time to PIVOT.

YOU are the LEADER.

Chapter 22

FORGIVENESS IS FREEDOM

Today, I am grateful to have learned so many lessons that have taught me and guided me through my life. Some lessons dealt out by Dick and Gwen were particularly harsh but lessons were learned because of the way I chose to deal with them.

While I have overcome many obstacles, I still struggle with personal challenges that life throws my way; just like anyone else. Unfortunately, I tend to go into a very quiet place and remove myself from most everyone in my life. It's not really depression but more like a way to protect myself which I believe stems from my early days of tragedy.

That quiet solitude habitually leads me into a process of assessment and reflection, and soon after, I have developed a plan. I am a problem-solver and this is how I tend to address most of my personal challenges.

I recognize the importance of being positive and sharing that with others. Peace of mind and inner peace is more possible when you resolve conflict and difficult situations. I am learning to meditate and want to learn how to meditate more deeply to help me assess myself and invite me to help others more freely.

Forgiveness is Freedom. Forgiveness is very important in all our lives. It allows us to shed our past and invites us to look positively to our future. Without forgiveness, we cannot be our whole selves. How can we give effectively to others without it?

After I became an adult, I learned that Dick suffered from manic depression and had been taking strong medications for several years as a result. This, in part, may explain his erratic behaviour towards us. Mental health is so critically important to understand and to be empathetic towards those who suffer any form of it.

Dick passed away October 27, 2010. I was in Italy at the time of his passing, and was not aware until I returned. I would have attended his service and being the orator of the family, would have at least shared some words had I been there. Interestingly, his obituary named the Pierson kids who were legally adopted as Barendregt children as "extended family." I doubt Dick would have liked that but nonetheless, it was done.

Dick suffered from dementia and had been separated from Gwen years earlier so was pretty much alone in a seniors home. I found it sad to be honest that in his end, he was alone for the most part. His words flowed back to my mind when I approached him to be a grandfather to my children: "I don't think I need anybody else in my family."

I forgive Dick. Our past was a big part of my life and my forgiving sets us both free.

Gwen, I have been told never wanted the adoption in the first place. I never asked her that and so I am perhaps unfairly stating this. Both Dick and Gwen were physically and emotionally abusive. So much so, I would guess they would never be allowed as adoptive parents in today's system. At least I would hope not.

Nonetheless, I forgive Gwen too. I have thought for many years on this matter and to be honest, I just didn't think it possible to forgive her, but I can. If she had been asked to take on the adoption against her own will, that is also unfair to her. It was most certainly a lot to ask of anyone and regrettably, they should have thought it out more. For both Dick and Gwen, I feel they missed the opportunity to share in all the love and happiness us Pierson kids would have brought them in the end.

As for Dick and Gwen's children, Mike, Cheryl and Susan. I have come to appreciate just how their lives had changed when we came into their family. They too, were victims in some ways. They didn't have a say in it. While we are mostly not close, we all have a connection. I especially keep in touch with Mike and have so appreciated our rekindled bond the last five or six years. There is nothing to forgive with them; only love and respect.

EPILOGUE

One of the most unselfish things our mother did for us six kids was to have written a letter to each of us before she died. How difficult that must have been for her? She was a thirty-one year-old Mother of six, leaving her precious children behind so abruptly. When Mom died, the oldest of her children was twelve years old; the youngest only five. Cancer had ravaged her body; just as it had caused her mother's death when she was only five. Death was the only release from the pain. She had hung on longer than expected because of her children.

Mom's handwriting was so beautifully artistic. Her cursive writing danced. Her letter means something different to each of us six kids. To me, it was inspirational.

She wrote:

To My Darling Children

I am writing this letter to you now so I'll be sure of your getting it when the right time comes. Today, I feel fine and wish all of you could come to see me. This is our last goodbye and I hope I can say everything in this letter that is in my heart. Most of all, please don't forget me. In some little way, find something to remember me by. Always try to remember the Lord works in funny ways and right now I find it hard to understand why he is separating us.

Now, you will be taking on a new chapter in life because you see life is something like reading a book. After you read so many pages, you go onto a new chapter and this part of your life is a new chapter. The first part was with me and Lord, I wouldn't have traded you guys for anything. I had about as much love for you six kids as I could hold. All of you were my life and now it has to stop.

You Gordie are a very responsible person and very headstrong. Stay that way boy and in life you will gain and always keep my love with you.

Billie, The Nature Boy. Do you suppose we shall ever curb your nasty temper? You have a wonderful gift Bill. That is having a way with words. Try hard to put them to good use and keep working on your doctor plan. Bill, carry my love with you always and life shall be good to you.

My one and only Susan. At least we went through life far enough to have our talk. Remember it well Sue and thank you for the love you gave me out of life. It was harder for you than the rest as you and I were outnumbered. Sue, you were a beautiful daughter and you're a hard worker in every way. Just take enough time to think things over and remember all through life what we talked about because, like all the boys, I want you to get the best out of life. Susie, try so very hard to remember me.

Hi Dan! I imagine this will be (the) worst shock to you as you have sort of been alone and withdrawn from everyone else. Try to stay an honest boy Dannie and always remember if you tell the truth nothing is as bad in the end. Remember to always wear that beautiful smile of yours and let everyone see those beautiful dimples you have. Remember that I loved you very much and try to remember me a little.

Hi to Stevie, "My Funny Clown". You are a funny boy Stevie. I loved you for it as one of the nicest things in the world is to make other people happy, but sometimes you have to understand not everything is funny.

Now Larrie. I guess you will always be the baby as being the youngest you got most of the attention and mostly spoiled. You are a happy boy and may God keep you that way but always try to be good and think of other people.

My Darling children, this is sort of my last goodbye to you and to assure you of my love for you. I'm so sorry God chose to separate us as a family but maybe he has a little better future planned for you. Jack is going to raise you now because he loves you and doesn't want to see you separated from one another and when times get rough and hard, remember it is hard for him too. But even if it's only

Epilogue

for my memory; try to pull it together because it is my wish. Good bye to all of my Darlings, be brave & strong.

With all my Strongest Love,

Mommy

(Just a footnote: Jack was the man who was living with us at the time of mom's death and had been her boyfriend for a period of time. I'm not sure how long that was. Jack never made good on his promise to take care of us. In fact, I would dare say he looked after us more than a few days before we went back to the orphanage after Mom passed.)

This letter motivated me throughout my entire life. I keep the original handwritten letter in my safekeeping and often pull it out to read, and just adore Mom's handwriting.

I have run my hands over the pages many times to try to feel her energy or a whiff of her fragrance. In many ways, Mom's letter helped me through some difficult periods of my life. I expect this is what she set out to achieve.

It's uncanny how she was able to understand mine and my sibling's characters in the message she left for each of us. In my opinion, her insight about each of us at our tender ages reflected rather accurately each of our personalities in our adult years.

Each time when I felt like giving up, I was motivated by her words.

I was moved to try harder; to make her proud of me. Even now, I find inspiration from reading her words.

And just to come full circle, a short note to my mom, who was my invisible guide throughout my life. Never underestimate the effect that your kindness can have on someone, how your belief in them may be just enough to make them see in themselves what you have seen. We can all make a difference.

And so, in closing:

Dear Mom,

I have quietly spoken many letters to you over the years through my thoughts and prayers. My words spoken as a child, an adolescent, and then as an adult have perhaps changed over the years but the same theme always sticks no matter what. I miss you. There are many feelings in those three words. I think you know that. I have felt your presence from time to time, but never enough to satisfy my yearning to feel your warm hugs, soft hands, and of course, a kiss that always made everything better.

I want to thank you for writing this letter to us six kids. It has served me well over the last fifty-plus years. Your words that dance across the baby blue iridescent pages inspired me to know I deserved better in my life. Mom, you set the standard for me from the moment I was able to develop a memory with you. I felt your love for me had no bounds and despite your leaving my life so early, it was enough perhaps to guide me and protect me from what you may have known would come into my life after you left.

As I write this book, it has taught me that resilience comes from difficulties as long as we've learned lessons along the way. You leaving me so early was the most difficult challenge in my life but the love you gave me was just enough to support those challenges. I hope you are proud of what I've been able to accomplish because you were my inspiration for many of my successes.

I love you mommy. I always have. I always will.

Love from your "funny clown", Stevie.

ACKNOWLEDGEMENTS

First to my loving wife Sandra who without her support and convincing to finally write this book may never have happened. You inspire me everyday.

To my children; all of whom have heard snippets of my stories over their years. I hope this book provides clarity and inspiration for you to dream bigger. I adore you all.

To the special people whom, through different phases of my life, have made a difference to me. I am forever grateful and deeply love and respect you:

The late John Henry (Jack) Pfeffer and Joyce (mother) Pfeffer and their beautiful family; all of whom I consider my family and my siblings. A special love and respect to Ken Pfeffer who features prominently in my book as my childhood friend and a brother to me today.

To John and Diane Verbruggen who taught me many lessons; not the least of which was hard work and accountability.

To the late (Michael) Punch Kent who inspired me to dream bigger and believe in myself.

To Bill and Valerie Cron. You both taught me so many lessons that I only realized after many years but lessons that I admire and share with others now; the least of which is do unto others as you would have them do unto you.

To Mr. Howard Branscombe, my high school principal who fostered my early leadership in carving a path for me to choose.

ABOUT THE AUTHOR

Steve has spent more than 35 years as an entrepreneur and has held progressively senior roles within the financial services sector.

What led Steve to a fulfilling career and becoming a seasoned **Coach, Mentor and Leader** is a TRUE story of **resilience, faith and a belief** that he deserved better having lived through the traumas he faced from his early years in the orphanage and the years that followed.

Steve is involved in his community; having served as a volunteer, past president of the board and committee member with several organizations including Georgian College, RVH, Season's Centre for Grieving Children, and a past member of Rotary Canada.

He resides in Barrie, Ontario with his wife Sandra and their two dogs, Pierson and Oscar. Lovingly supported by his children and grandchildren, they spend much of their time at their cottage in Burks Falls, Ontario.

You can connect with Steve here www.bookstomotivate.com and LinkedIn: www.linkedin.com/in/steven-barendregt-author-4ab9b63a

BOOK STEVE TO SPEAK

Book Steve as your next Keynote speaker. You're Guaranteed to be Inspired, Motivated and Moved.

Combining more than 35 years as an entrepreneur and senior leader within the financial services sector, Steve's talks are inspiring.

With his TRUE raw accounting of an upbringing that many of us can't even fathom, he recounts the many hardships growing up and how it helped shape him into the effective coach, mentor, and leader he is today.

Steve's vulnerable sharing of the traumas that bind us as humans are thought-provoking and push us to be our better selves. Combined with his natural humour that resonates with his audiences, he *influences* listeners into thinking more positively and succeeding despite the challenges we may face in our lives.

You may feel you're on the outside right now, but you're about to be let in!

To learn more, contact Steve here: www.bookstomotivate.com/contact

www.ingramcontent.com/pod-product-compliance
Lightning Source LLC
Chambersburg PA
CBHW072050110526
44590CB00018B/3111